On Your Bike
in
The Chilterns

Sue and Paul Thomas

COUNTRYSIDE BOOKS
NEWBURY BERKSHIRE

COUNTRYSIDE BOOKS
3 Catherine Road
Newbury, Berkshire

To view our complete range of books,
please visit us at
www.countrysidebooks.co.uk

ISBN 1 85306 664 8

Designed by Graham Whiteman
Maps by the authors and redrawn by
Gelder design and mapping
Photographs by Paul Thomas unless otherwise stated

Produced through MRM Associates Ltd., Reading
Printed by Cambridge University Press

CONTENTS

AREA MAP SHOWING THE LOCATIONS OF THE RIDES

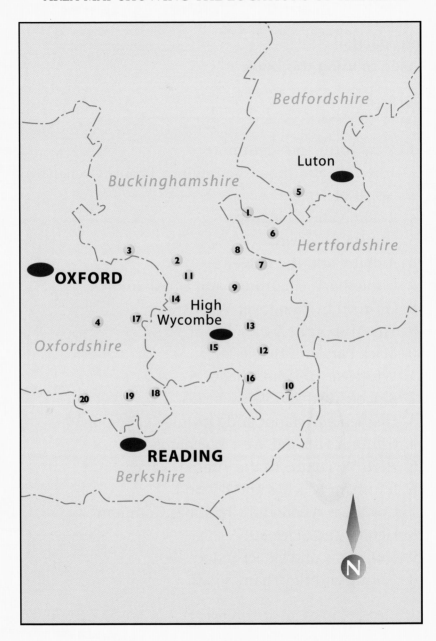

INTRODUCTION

Within easy reach of London, it is often difficult to believe you are so close to the Metropolis while cycling through the quiet lanes and woodlands of the Chilterns. These chalk hills are deservedly classed as an Area of Outstanding Natural Beauty (AONB) and in contrast to our heavily visited National Parks offer surprising solitude and that often needed escape.

Modest hills these may be, but they can still be steep and supply demanding climbs and exhilarating descents. Aimed at the leisure cyclist, the routes in this guide will avoid the excesses, but it will not be flat – so don't be deceived by short distances! And remember, a 5 mile off-road route is easy if taken slowly (walking up hills and avoiding obstacles) but ride at cross country competition pace and it will be hard, so pace yourself.

The rides consist of 20 routes of varying length, between 2½ and 24½ miles, aimed at the family and leisure cyclist, rather than the hardened enthusiast. However, the routes are close enough together to allow them to be linked to provide longer runs for the more ambitious, giving a good introduction for cyclists new to the area. They range from the picturesque village of Aldbury and the Ridgeway to off-road cycle trails in Wendover Woods, from the bustle of Henley on Thames to Burnham Beeches and beyond. There is something for everyone, with the best of the Chilterns on display here.

The routes have been numbered to fall into four main categories. The first, routes 1 to 4, covers the Aylesbury Vale and the Oxfordshire Plain: flatter ground below, and with views of, the Chiltern escarpment. The second, routes 5 to 9, covers the Northern Chilterns, the hills north of the Misbourne and the Wendover Gap. Routes 10 to 15 are in the Central Chilterns, between the Misbourne and the M40, and the last group, routes 16 to 20, falls within the Southern Chilterns, from the M40 to the Thames.

The Chilterns have something to offer in all seasons, but perhaps the most scenic are spring with the woodlands carpeted in bluebells, and autumn when the leaves turn to gold. Whenever you choose to take a ride, take your time and enjoy the journey along with the attractions on the way.

Sue and Paul Thomas

GUIDE TO USING THIS BOOK

Each route is preceded by information to help you:

The **number of miles** is indicated and is the total that you will cover excluding detours. Distances are 'map-measured'.

The brief **introduction** to the ride gives a broad picture of where the route takes you and also mentions particular features you will see.

The **maps** listed at the beginning of each ride are all Ordnance Survey maps and it is advisable to take them with you as the sketch maps give limited information. The OS maps at 1:50000 (Landranger) and 1:25000 (Explorer) are the best for cycling, and the wealth of information on the Explorer sheets makes them the preferred choice. Three Explorer sheets cover most of the area and these are Chiltern Hills North, Chiltern Hills West and Chiltern Hills East. Note that only at the end of the last century did Explorer become the standard 1:25000 map, prior to that the standard was the smaller area Pathfinder map, with Explorers only available for certain popular areas. Under this scheme there there were two Chiltern Hills maps, North and South – maps number 2 and 3. This guide refers only to the new series maps, but if you have the old series they may be usable for a particular route. The old and new North sheets are roughly equivalent, as is the combined new East and West and the old double-sided South sheet. However, in both cases the new sheets cover slightly more ground.

All routes have a **starting point** where parking is available, and where possible are near a rail station. Where a station is not close to the described starting point, one is usually nearby at some point on the route, and this is highlighted in the description. All of the rail operators covering the lines relevant to this guide allow bikes to be carried free of charge, and normally without pre-booking, but not during the rush hours from and into London. Tandems, trikes and other larger cycles are not usually allowed. Regulations do vary, so call and check with the station before setting out.

Places for refreshment are mentioned in the pre-ride information and others are just waiting for you to discover them. Don't forget Paragraph 211 of the Highway Code: You MUST NOT ride under the influence of drink or drugs.

THE ROUTES

It is a good idea to read right through a route before setting out so that you note any places where you want to spend more time. Remember, things can change, pubs close, off-road tracks deteriorate – others are repaired. So be prepared, while every care has been taken to ensure accuracy, things may not be quite as advertised!

The route directions have been made as brief as possible, while still being readable. The intention is that you should be able to read and hold a fragment of description in your mind between landmarks. Safety warnings, eg busy road crossings, are shown in bold type. Instructions to turn left or right are also printed in bold, like this: **Turn L** at the T-junction. Instructions to continue straight over a crossroads or carry straight on are not in bold.

Following the directions are details of the major **places of interest** you will encounter on your ride. There is so much to do and see in this area that not everything can be included here, and further notable attractions may be mentioned in the route introduction, others are left for you to discover.

A **sketch map** accompanies each route description. Whilst it should be possible to follow the routes using just this guide, it is recommended that you also carry a more detailed map. This will add to your enjoyment, and help should you stray from the route. Note that the sketch maps are not to scale, and the scale varies, with complicated areas requiring more detail at a larger scale. Also, to aid usability, not all detail is shown, only that which helps in following the route.

BEFORE YOU START

The routes in this guide avoid off-road tracks that are poor during winter, and so are suitable all year round. If you are planning to explore other bridleways, remember they can be very muddy in winter and become overgrown in summer, often being at their best in the autumn and early spring. Remember that cycling off-road on footpaths is not allowed. If you do explore stick to bridleways, byways and RUPPs (Roads Used as Public Paths), or other routes where cycling is clearly indicated as being allowed.

Make sure your bike is well maintained and safe, it is easier than trying to fix a broken bike miles from anywhere. There are, however, repairs you need to be prepared for, the main one being a puncture. The chance of a puncture can be reduced by ensuring tyres are not under inflated, but especially off-road you will eventually succumb. So, carry a spare tube, tyre levers, and a small pump; it is also worth carrying instant repair patches should you have more than one puncture to deal with.

After punctures, the most common problems relate to things coming loose, the chain breaking, frayed cables snapping, or spokes breaking. Good maintenance will prevent all. These things are not frequent occurrences, so don't be put off, but for peace of mind you may want to look at the various multi-tools on the market. These are very compact and light, and can handle most emergency jobs. A bicycle maintenance book, Haynes do a very good one, will explain how to effect repairs and show you how to do at least the more simple maintenance jobs on your bike and will quickly pay for itself.

There are various bag and pannier systems available to carry your tools and spares, together with food, camera, spare clothing etc. This is easier and less restrictive than using a rucksack, though this is very much a matter of personal preference. Bottle cages will carry your water bottles; remember to take enough and refill as required, on a hot summer's day dehydration can start surprisingly quickly.

Clothing needs to be non-restrictive and comfortable, and there should be nothing loose to become entangled with moving parts. There are two pieces of specialist cycling gear you may want to consider from the outset. Firstly, padded cycling shorts can make a great difference to comfort on a day in the saddle. Secondly, waterproofs; good, breathable, waterproofs are a must unless you are sure of fine weather (in England?). Cycling-specific versions are cut to cover the lower back without getting in the way when dismounting, but any good breathable fabric jacket will suffice.

A cycling helmet is recommended. There is much debate around this subject and helmet use is not compulsory, but there is evidence that helmets do reduce the severity of

injuries sustained and save lives. We always wear ours.

SAFETY

Being close to large centres of population you will come across traffic even on quiet lanes, and occasionally the routes in this guide by necessity follow or cross busier roads – though these are avoided wherever possible. It is important that you know how to cycle in traffic; remember, ride confidently, and if necessary walk your bike on the pavement. Any potentially busy roads and crossings are highlighted in the text, please take extra care at these points.

Key to Sketch Maps

⌐⌐	Road	)(	Bridge
------	Track or Bridleway	!	Extra Care
·········	Shared use Path	▯	Pub
—•—	Railway & Station	⌂	Church
←	Direction of Route	☀	Viewpoint
START	Start of Route	▪	Notable Building
P	Parking	✗	Windmill

1

Marsworth and Mentmore

19 miles

This ride is almost exclusively on quiet country lanes, with exceptional views and starts from a very scenic and popular spot on the Grand Union Canal. The route begins with three canal crossings, where the Aylesbury arm meets the main course and then heads away from the Chilterns before climbing to a series of magnificent views. The most notable is to be seen from the Aston Abbotts to Weedon road, where the route takes a brief detour, so don't skip this.

Map: OS Landranger 165 Aylesbury and Leighton Buzzard or OS Explorer 181 and 192 (GR 919141).

Starting point: The route starts from the British Waterways Startop's car park in Marsworth, on the B489 near Tring. This is a very popular spot, so arrive early on summer Sundays and Bank Holidays.

By train: Cheddington station, on the London Euston to Birmingham line, is just off route and gives a good public transport start point. From the station turn right to join the route in Cheddington at a mini-roundabout.

Refreshments: There are two pubs just opposite the car park, the Anglers Retreat and the White Lion, which is actually on the canal side. Most of the villages passed on the route have inviting looking pubs, but if you can wait the Stag in Mentmore is recommended, and it is an easy run home from this point.

The route: Small hills but big views over the Aylesbury Vale more than compensate for the moderate exertion required on this ride.

Turn **L** out of the car park, and just past the Anglers Retreat, **turn R** onto Watery Lane. After a sharp right bend cross two arms of the canal. On arriving at a junction by the church **turn L** and pass the Red Lion on the right before crossing the canal again. Stay with the road through sharp bends to a 'Give Way' sign, where **turn R** heading for Long Marston and Wingrave.

Go through Long Marston, passing a

crossroads, two pubs and a shop whilst still heading for Wingrave. On entering Wingrave **turn L** onto Lower End to complete the climb into the village by a back street. Note the views to the left back to the Chiltern escarpment. Pass the church on the left, and **turn L** at the junction. **Keep L** and then **R** as the road winds through the village to arrive at a junction with the **busy A418**, where **turn L** and then immediately **R** heading for Aston Abbotts.

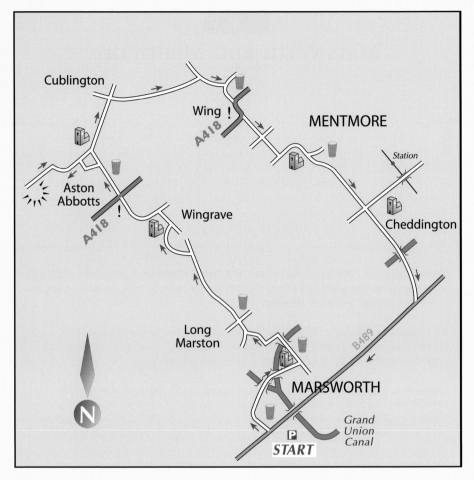

In Aston Abbotts pass the Royal Oak and Bull and Butcher pubs, to arrive at a junction on a right-hand bend. **Turn L** here signed for Weedon, gated road. Follow this road through the gate on a left-hand bend by a row of houses, to a bench by a public footpath where the road starts to descend. Admire the views from this point, to the left the Chilterns, ahead Aylesbury, and to the right Aylesbury Vale. Then return to the junction in Aston Abbotts.

Turn L now, passing the church, and heading for Cublington. At the 'Give Way' in Cublington, **turn R** on the Wing road. A long fast stretch leads to another 'Give Way' on the edge of Wing, where **turn R** onto a busier road, and after a short climb **turn R** again onto the High Street signed for Aylesbury. Pass pubs and shops to meet the A418 on a sharp bend, **turn R** onto the 'A' road, and almost immediately leave the road to the L on a sharp right bend.

Descend through open fields, with glimpses of Mentmore Towers in the woods ahead, to a 'Give Way' at a

Looking towards the Chiltern escarpment from Aston Abbotts

crossroads where go straight ahead. **Keep L** with the road where a 'no through road' goes to the right, and then a short climb leads up past the church to a junction in Mentmore. **Keep R** and pass the Stag, before descending the tree-lined avenue to a double mini-roundabout in Cheddington. A left here leads back to the station if you came by train, but continue straight ahead to pass through Cheddington. At the traffic lights, cross the canal with the canal basin, boat trips and a cafe on the left and the Duke of Wellington pub on the right.

At the 'Give Way' **turn R** on the 'B' road heading back for Marsworth, cross the canal again at the traffic lights by the White Horse and the car park is immediately on the left.

THE GRAND UNION CANAL

The Grand Union Canal provides an interesting and diverse attraction, with reservoirs and nature reserves along its route, much of which is cycleable with a permit from British Waterways. The canal links London to Birmingham, and climbs to a height of 430 ft at its summit in the Chilterns. Water supply in these chalk hills has always been a problem, with a feeder arm from Wendover being constructed but proving ineffective. By 1802, just a few years after opening, a system of pumps and reservoirs had to be installed, this route's starting point being a part of that legacy. Water loss and supply problems continued to plague the canal and in the drought of 1902 a borehole was needed at Cow Roast to maintain supplies. The canal remains popular today, but with leisure rather than industrial traffic.

The Grand Union Canal near Marsworth

MENTMORE

An estate village consisting of cottages situated along a green. The grand Victorian mansion of Mentmore Towers was built in the 1850s for Baron Meyer de Rothschild and is one of a series of properties built in the area by the Rothschild family, which includes Waddesdon Manor and Halton House. Interestingly, it has eight bathrooms on the first floor and was one of the first houses to have a hot water system and central heating via underfloor pipes. At the time of writing it is not open to the public.

AYLESBURY DUCK

Aylesbury Duck made Aylesbury famous, beginning as a cottage industry in the 19th century and using the many ponds and streams in the area to breed and rear the ducks, which were then exported all over the world. They are still bred but output has considerably declined since the Second World War.

Towersey and the Risborough to Thame Cycle Path

21½ miles

Quiet lanes, sleepy villages and a delightful converted railway track on the flattish lands north of Princes Risborough are among the attractions on this route. Princes Risborough sits at the foot of the Chiltern escarpment on the edge of the Aylesbury Vale. The return from Towersey takes in the converted Thame to Princes Risborough railway route, opened by Sustrans in late 2000 and now a popular cycle path.

Map: OS Landranger 165 Aylesbury and Leighton Buzzard or OS Explorer 181 (GR 805034).

Starting point: The route starts from The Mount pay and display car park by St Mary's church and the Leisure Centre, just off the High Street in Princes Risborough.

By train: Princes Risborough station is on the London Marylebone to Birmingham via High Wycombe line, and Monks Risborough is on a spur of this line to Aylesbury. Both stations are close to the start of the route.

Refreshments: Two pubs of note on this route are the Harrow at Bishopstone which offers food and a beer garden, and the Three Horseshoes at Towersey which has a large garden with children's play area.

The route: This sticks to the lower ground on peaceful country lanes and so is not at all strenuous. Should you intend to explore the bridleways and byways in this area, beware, as in winter deep mud can be a serious problem! Princes Risborough is a small town providing all the expected facilities, including a cycle shop with cycle hire.

From the car park follow Church Street, with the church on the left, to the Market Square to **turn L** at the High Street. At the roundabout go straight across (2nd exit including the supermarket) onto Longwick Road and after a short distance **turn first R** onto Wellington Avenue.

(Note: a shared-use cycle path on the left can be used to cross the roundabout if preferred, and this then continues alongside Longwick Road, crossing to the right just before Wellington Avenue.)

Follow this road through Monks

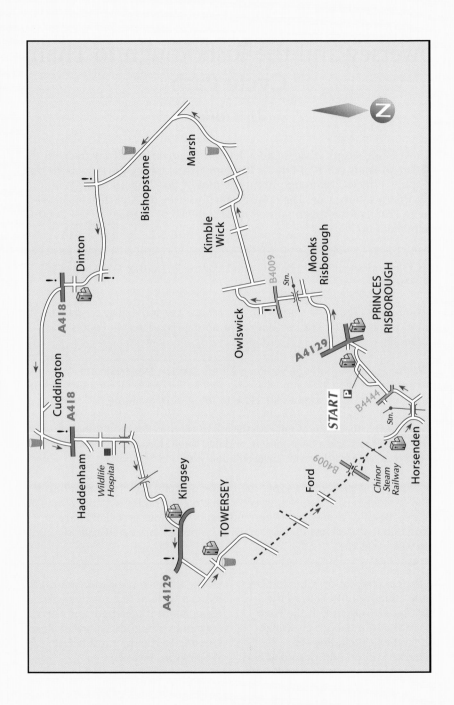

Risborough, **bearing first L** then **R** to emerge at a minor road where you **turn L** to pass under a railway bridge. Follow this lane until it ends at a T-junction with the B4009. **Turn L** here and then shortly **first R** signed for Owlswick. Pass a road on the left to Longwick, and keep with the road as it bears right through the hamlet of Owlswick. **Turn R** at the next junction and then **L** after passing Stockwell Lane Farm heading for Kimble Wick.

Kimble Wick Road is then followed through Kimble Wick, ignoring minor roads to the left and right. After two 90° bends proceed straight on at a staggered junction towards Marsh. **Keep L** where a road joins from the right by the Prince of Wales pub, and then **turn L** at the next junction to join the road into Bishopstone.

Pass the Harrow public house in Bishopstone and continue to a road junction with the minor but busy Portway Road. **Turn L**, signed Thame and Haddenham and follow this road **with care** for 1½ miles to another crossroads after a slight climb. **Turn R** here heading for Dinton.

After passing through the village, this road leads to a junction with the A418, **turn L** and then immediately **R** onto Cuddington Road, **taking care**, as this is a busy road. Follow the road into Cuddington, ignoring a minor left, to **turn L** at the crossroads in the centre of the village by the Crown pub. This leads downhill to cross the Dad Brook, before climbing back to the A418.

Turn L with care and immediately right onto The Churchway heading towards Haddenham. After ½ mile, and as the road bends to the right, **bear L**

keeping to the edge of Haddenham. At a 'Give Way' on a crossroads continue straight ahead to stay on Stanbridge Road. Pass the turn for the wildlife hospital and cross Stan Bridge, follow the road round a sharp right bend after a junction to the left. Several more sharp bends lead shortly into Kingsey and to the A4129.

Turn R with care and in ½ mile **L** onto Windmill Road heading for Towersey. **Turn L** at the end of the road into Towersey village and continue on to a crossroads, where go straight ahead, signed as a 'no through road'.

At the end of this road, in approximately ¾ mile, **turn R** on the private road to Penn Farm to reach the Thame to Risborough cycleway on the converted rail bed. **Turn L** here and continue on the cycleway to cross a bridleway and track at Hinton crossing, then to cross a minor road **with care**. Eventually reach a bridge over the road, after which descend to the right, then **turn L** onto the byway and cross the Chinnor Steam Railway by a level crossing.

Continue to a road, where you **turn R** to pass through Horsenden. At the junction **turn L** to cross the railway then **L again** on Picts Lane heading for Princes Risborough. At the 'Give Way' **turn L** and then very shortly **R** onto Manor Park Avenue. Where Stratton Road turns left signed for the town centre, continue on Manor Park Avenue, a private gated road, to return to the car park. Stratton Road also leads back to the car park should the gate be shut.

• •

Pond at Horsenden

PRINCES RISBOROUGH

Princes Risborough, originally Great Risborough, was renamed after the Black Prince who had a hunting lodge in the area. Nearby Monks Risborough, as the name suggests, was founded as a monastic settlement but is now a residential suburb of Princes Risborough.

Both settlements lie along the line of the Icknield Way at the base of the Chilterns. This has been an important trade route through much of the area's recorded past. Princes Risborough also sits in the mouth of a great gap in the Chiltern Hills (produced during the last Ice Age), which forms a route to High Wycombe via

16

Saunderton, and this also became a key transport link.

TOWERSEY

A village well known for its annual folk festival, one of the largest on the calendar, and also for its Morris dancers. They are well worth watching and are known for their rude traditional fertility songs.

ST TIGGYWINKLES

Europe's first wildlife teaching hospital was originally founded to care for injured hedgehogs. It is open to the public all year round and offers a visitor centre, souvenir shop and tea bar, and is just off this route in Haddenham. Next door there is a farm walk and picnic site also open all year.

CHINNOR STEAM RAILWAY

The railway runs between Chinnor and Princes Risborough parallel to the Icknield Way at the foot of the Chilterns and is crossed by this route. It is manned entirely by volunteers. Opening times vary but Bank Holidays and weekends often see the trains in steam.

North of Thame

24½ miles

A long and interesting route with extensive views and, once away from Thame and Long Crendon, very little traffic, passing through pretty villages such as Ludgershall, Brill, Worminghall and Oakley. Thame itself is a bustling little town with much history and interesting modern shops and well worth exploring before or after your ride.

Map: OS Landranger 165 Aylesbury and Leighton Buzzard or OS Explorer 180 (GR 707058).

Starting point: There is plenty of parking in the centre of Thame, although as this is a busy market town, finding a space on Saturdays can be tricky. The route is described as starting from the 'cattle market' long stay car park on North Street. There are public toilets by this car park.

By train: There is a rail station at Haddenham and Thame Parkway, a couple of miles out of Thame, on the edge of Haddenham. This is on the London Marylebone to Birmingham via High Wycombe line. If using the train it is best to join and leave this route via Cuddington, unless a visit to Thame is desired.

Refreshments: There are shops, pubs and restaurants in Thame. Of the pubs, the Rising Sun by the mini-roundabouts is good, and the Bird Cage is popular – and housed in a very interesting building. For something more substantial, the Italian restaurant on the High Street (Mia Capri) is recommended. Many of the villages on the route have pubs, and occasionally shops though few that would be open on a Sunday. Recommended stops are either the Bull and Butcher in Ludgershall or the Chandos Arms in Oakley.

The route: A surprisingly hilly circuit but well worth the extra effort required.

Leave the cattle market car park by either exit and **turn L** onto North Street, then, just before the High Street and a pedestrian crossing, **turn R** into the traffic-restricted Buttermarket. After a little way, **turn L** on the cobbled one-way system by the Town Hall and then **R** onto the High Street. At the mini-roundabouts continue straight ahead to stay on the High Street and pass the

16th century Old Trout hotel and restaurant.

At the end of the High Street, where the road bends sharp left, **turn R with care** onto Priestend. Pass the Prebendal on the left, and then the church on the right. Follow the road as it bears left and pass onto the now gated old road over Thame Bridge and the Bucks-

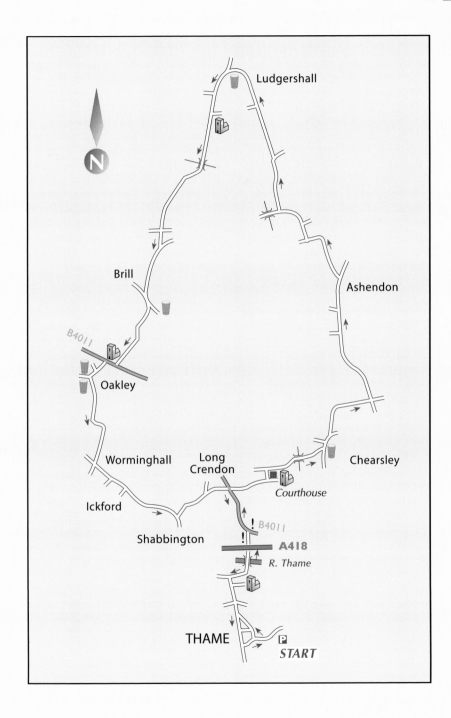

Oxon county boundary. Where the road meets the busy A418 Thame bypass, dismount and **cross with care** to join the continuation of the old road. Follow this to pass by another gate and Mead Farm, to a junction with the B4011, where you **turn L** heading for Long Crendon.

After climbing into Long Crendon, **turn R** at the first crossroads, signed 'village roads only' and follow the road as it winds through the pretty village High Street. Just past the Eight Bells pub and just before the church and 15th century courthouse surrounding the tiny Church Green, **turn L** at the 'no through road' sign. Then, at the T-junction **turn R** towards Chearsley.

A long descent followed by a stiff little climb leads to Chearsley. Follow the road through the village, passing the Bell on the right. **Turn L** onto Winchendon Road, signed for Waddesdon, where the main road bends right. Continue climbing through a sharp right bend to a crossroads at the top of the hill, where you **turn L** and then descend once more before climbing to Ashendon. Ignore minor left turns for Lower and Upper Pollicott, and **turn L** at the top of the hill, signed for Dorton and Brill. Make a steep descent to Wotton Underwood and a sharp left bend.

A little less than a mile on from the bend **turn R** for Brill and Ludgershall by a small wood. Ignore the right turn for Wotton only, and take the **next R**, just before a railway bridge. At the next junction, where the road bends sharply right, **turn L** to arrive in Ludgershall. Follow the road into the village, ignoring a left for Brill. By the village green and the Bull and Butcher public

house the road swings round to almost double back on itself. Ignore right turns first for Bicester and then Piddington to leave the village, passing by the church and heading now once more for Brill.

After 1½ miles, pass through a crossroad to a 'Give Way' where you **turn R** to climb into Brill. **Turn R** in Brill by the monument and green and descend to Oakley with extensive views on route. At a T-junction with the B4011 **turn R** onto the Bicester road, and shortly **L** after passing the church, signed for Worminghall. Look out for a small turn on the right to the Chandos Arms if a stop here is desired.

Turn L again by the garage, shop and Royal Oak public house still heading for Worminghall, where you **turn L** for Ickford, now following part of the Oxfordshire Cycleway. Ignore right-hand turns into Ickford village and follow the road to Shabbington, where you **turn L** at the top of a short climb onto Crendon Road.

On entering Long Crendon **turn R** onto Frogmore Lane and make one last climb to reach the B4011. **Turn R** and retrace the route followed on the outward journey to Thame, being careful not to miss the right-hand turn just past the golf driving range onto the old road by Mead Farm – **take care as this is a busy road**.

After passing the church, note the old tithe barn (now offices) across the allotments; **turn L** once on the High Street and opposite the Six Bells pub for a closer look. Note that the route cannot be retraced exactly through Thame due to the one-way system, so keep with the High Street and **turn L**

The old Thame Bridge

at the roundabout signed to the long stay parking and opposite the Black Horse.

● ●

LONG CRENDON COURTHOUSE

One of the first buildings to be acquired by the National Trust in 1900. Made partly of timber, it was built in the 15th century and thought to be initially used as a wool store, before taking up its role as a courthouse during the reign of Henry V. Still in the hands of the National Trust the upper floor only is open to the public, mainly at weekends and holidays during the summer.

OXFORDSHIRE CYCLEWAY

The Oxfordshire Cycleway is a varied and picturesque cycle route covering over 200 miles of mainly minor country roads and lanes. The route takes in Oxford City and its historic University buildings, Oxfordshire's Cotswolds, the Chiltern Hills and the Ridgeway, along with the important valleys and rivers in the area and their associated settlements. Route details describing the cycleway as a combination of six circular route options can be obtained from the Countryside Service, at Oxfordshire County Council.

THAME

Thame is an ancient market town full of colourful and interesting buildings ranging from the grand church to the many pubs and coaching inns. The old Grammar School at the north end of the High Street, built in 1569, was responsible for the education of Milton and John Hampden amongst others. Near to the school is the house where John Hampden died after being wounded at the battle of Chalgrove Field (see route 4). The annual Thame Show and its accompanying street fair echoes a time when the grander medieval show and fair filled the streets of this market town.

Ewelme and Chalgrove

16 miles

Adelightfully quiet route, starting on the Chiltern escarpment before sweeping down into the lowlands below to visit a monument to one of the Chilterns' most famous sons, by the site of the equally famous Civil War battle of Chalgrove Field. The return via Ewelme with its watercress beds and historic school is equally fascinating.

Map: OS Landranger 175 Reading and Windsor and 165 Aylesbury and Leighton Buzzard or OS Explorer 171 (GR 683902).

Starting point: Start from the car parking by St Botolph's 11th century church at Swyncombe, best approached from the B481 in Cookley Green. There are no facilities at the start.

By train: No railway stations are very convenient, but from Cholsey (one stop up from Goring, see route 20) this route can be joined at Ewelme, via Wallingford in 6½ miles.

Refreshments: The most natural breakpoint in this route is Chalgrove. The two recommended pubs are the Lamb, a popular brewery-owned music venue pub serving food all day and with a pleasant garden, and the Red Lion, more up-market serving excellent food and also with a small garden.

The route: This is a moderate to easy circuit.

Climb back up from the church to the road, where you **turn R** signed for Cookley Green. At Cookley Green, follow the road round to the right, then **turn L** at the 'Give Way'. Follow the B481 for ½ mile. Just after a right-hand turn for Stonor and Christmas Common, **turn L** signed for Britwell Salome.

The going is fast now, down Britwell Hill with extensive views, crossing the Ridgeway and Icknield Way before a slight climb, into Britwell Salome. Take the **first L** on entering Britwell Salome,

pass the cricket pavilion on the right to meet a busier road, where you **turn L**. In about ½ mile, at the top of a small rise, **turn R** for Brightwell Baldwin and Cuxham with views of Didcot power station to the left.

After passing through Upperton, **turn R** at a junction, still heading for Brightwell Baldwin. At a sharp right bend opposite Brightwell Barn, **turn L** onto a minor road marked 'unsuitable for motors'. Pass the private road sign and follow the bridleway throughout, past Cadwell Farm, to arrive at the road

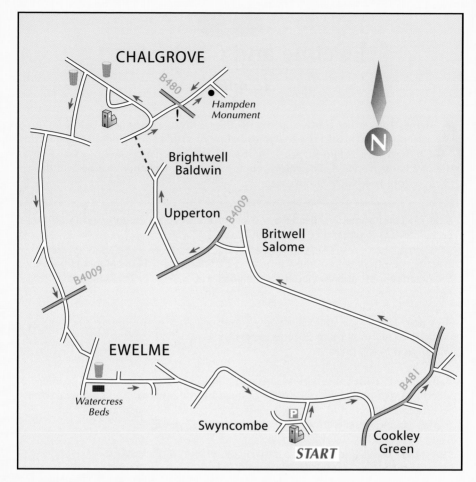

CHALGROVE

B480

Hampden Monument

Brightwell Baldwin

Upperton

B4009

Britwell Salome

B4009

EWELME

Watercress Beds

Swyncombe

P

START

B481

Cookley Green

N

on the edge of Chalgrove, where you **turn R.**

Turn R at the junction over the small bridge onto Monument Road. At the junction with the B480, **turn R**, then immediately **L** by Chalgrove Airfield, **take care.** Note Chalgrove Field on the left, and shortly on the right, the Hampden Monument.

After visiting this historic spot, return by Monument Road towards Chalgrove. Re-cross the B480, **keep R** at the junction visited earlier, and

shortly **turn L** onto Church Lane, following the signs for the church, to visit the parish church of St Mary. **Turn L** out of the church grounds to return to the main road through the village, where you **turn L.** Pass pubs and shops, including the Red Lion on the right, through Chalgrove's mix of old and new housing.

At a junction with Mill Lane, **turn L** by the Lamb public house. Pass the old watermill on the left and **turn R** at the junction for Berrick Salome, and shortly **L** for Ewelme. Ignore a right turn and at

The Red Lion serves excellent food

the junction with the B4009 go straight ahead. At a junction on the bend **keep L**. **Turn R** at the next junction, then **L** by the Shepherds Hut public house, passing the watercress beds on the right. At the junction by the pond keep with the road signed for Swyncombe.

Where the road bends right, **turn L** passing the impressive and historic Ewelme School. Keep straight on where a road joins from the left. Then **turn L** signed for Swyncombe at the next junction. At a sharp right-hand bend continue with the road, where the Swans Way bridleway goes straight ahead. Pass Lower Farm and Lower Cottages before the final steep climb back to the road to Swyncombe church. **Turn R** and descend back to the church.

JOHN HAMPDEN

John Hampden, who plays an important role in this route, is commemorated by the Hampden Monument which was erected in his honour. It was here that he first raised arms against the King and was subsequently mortally wounded in 1643 by the Royalists led by Prince Rupert. This was the battle of Chalgrove Field, and Colonel John Hampden, the Chiltern man, became the first champion of Parliament to battle against Charles I.

EWELME

Ewelme Watercress Beds fell into disrepair in the mid 1980s and are now the subject of a Chiltern Society conservation project. Maintenance work is ongoing but the area is now open to the general public and in 2004, a new visitor centre was opened on the site of the old watercress packing shed. Guided walks are available from the Watercress Centre.

Swyncombe church

The other notable thing about Ewelme is that its churchyard is the site of the grave of Jerome K. Jerome, who was the author of *Three Men in a Boat*. He lived in the village for a short time in the 1880s and his ashes were buried there in 1927. The village also boasts the oldest church school in England still in use (founded in 1437).

SWYNCOMBE

Swyncombe is made up from the old English name of 'swin', meaning wild boar, and 'cumb', a valley in the flank of the hill. It is thought to be an area where wild boars were hunted. St Botolph's church is believed to be of Norman origin and houses examples of needlework, a craft which has been carried out by its parishioners for many years. An exciting discovery was made in the 19th century when restoration work uncovered a previously unknown window on the north side.

5

Dunstable Downs

18 miles

This route offers peaceful lanes and gentle gradients among the rolling arable fields on the dip slope behind the Downs. The Dunstable Downs are very popular, and the starting point for this ride is no exception, with its easily accessible extensive views. On summer Sundays this piece of the Downs is alive with kite flyers, walkers and picnickers. Below is the London Gliding Club and the Downs offer a good vantage point to watch the gliders being catapulted or towed into the air. Once away from the car park, the crowds are quickly left behind and with no major tourist attractions on the route this is a pleasantly quiet ride through agricultural land, a patchwork of woodland and arable fields dissected by winding lanes and rich hedgerows.

Map: OS Landranger 166 Luton and Hertford or OS Explorer 181 and 182 (GR 008198).

Starting point: The popular Dunstable Downs car park on the B4541, a short drive from Dunstable. There is a National Trust shop and exhibition by the car park, where snacks and gifts can be bought; there are also toilets.

By train: There is no railway station convenient for this route.

Refreshments: Several pubs are passed en route, the Old Chequers in Gaddesden Row, and the Farmers Boy in Kensworth being recommended.

The route: The gradients encountered are generally gentle, with a long descent on the outward run to Gaddesden Row, and a long gradual climb back onto the Downs from Markyate on the return. The steepest climbs are quite short, and out of small intervening valleys.

Turn R out of the car park, ignore the minor left by the monument, and after a slight climb descend to a roundabout, where go straight on heading for Studham. After approximately 1½ miles, go straight on at the crossroads in Studham. Climb to another crossroads and go straight on. Shortly after this, where the road bends sharp right, **turn L** onto a more minor road heading for Gaddesden Row.

After 1 mile, enter Gaddesden Row and **bear L** with the road, signed for Stags End. Ignore a minor left then right in the dip, pass a water tower on the right and after passing a further minor left then right, the Old Chequers pub.

At the junction at the end of

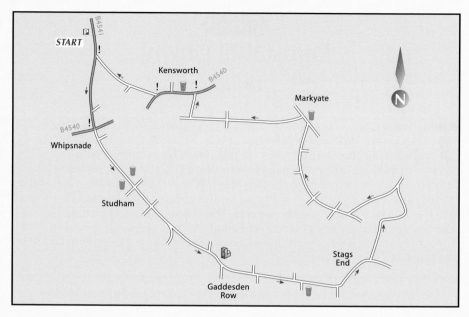

Gaddesden Row **bear L** with the road signed for Redbourn, then approximately ½ mile after passing Stags End equestrian centre **turn L** onto a narrow lane. Climb past Green Lane Farm, then through a sharp right followed by a sharp left turn to a short descent to a junction. **Turn sharp L.**

Climb, and after passing Puddephats Farm, **keep R** where a track joins from the left. At the next junction with a more major road go straight ahead, and maintain the same general direction. Go straight ahead at a crossroads by Beechwood House School. Two climbs and two descents then lead to Markyate where **turn L**, and immediately **L again** by the fire station and opposite the Sun Inn heading for Whipsnade.

A gradual climb leads away from Markyate and to a crossroads, where you go straight ahead. In ¾ mile **turn R** onto the traffic-restricted Dovehouse

The village pub at Studham

Far reaching views from Dunstable Downs

Lane. In Kensworth **turn L**, pass the Farmers Boy pub, and just after the right for Church End, where the road bends to the left, **turn R** on a minor road. Follow the lane passing the Isle of Wight nurseries to arrive back at the junction by the monument.

• •

DUNSTABLE DOWNS

Dunstable Downs provide a home for a rich variety of flora and fauna, and have a high point of 798 feet above sea level. There is much history and archaeology to explore along the Downs, with Bronze Age burial mounds, medieval rabbit warrens and Roman theatres. Visit the exhibition centre for more details together with information leaflets and maps.

WHIPSNADE

Whipsnade is close to this route and is the home of Whipsnade Wildlife Park. This is a part of the Zoological Society of London, a major wildlife conservation charity concerned with breeding, fieldwork and reintroductions. The park can be spotted from a distance by the lion that was cut into the hillside in the early 1930s to advertise what was then Whipsnade Zoo. Whipsnade is also known for its tree cathedral, also originating in the 1930s. Different varieties of trees were planted to make up the cathedral shape for this war memorial, now owned by the National Trust.

Aldbury and the Ridgeway

16 miles

After passing through the picture postcard village of Aldbury, the Grand Union Canal is crossed before climbing to Wigginton. Here the route goes off-road following the Icknield Way Riders' Route through Tring Park, then Hastoe and Pavis Woods. A steep downhill then heads into Tring with minor roads leading back to our starting point.

Map: OS Landranger 165 Aylesbury and Leighton Buzzard or OS Explorer 181 (GR 954148).

Starting point: The car park at Pitstone Hill, just off the B488 Tring to Dunstable road.

By train: Tring station is on the London Euston, Watford, Hemel Hempstead and Northampton line. The route passes by the railway station.

Refreshments: Tring is a small town with all facilities. Along the way attractive pubs will be found in the villages of Aldbury, Wigginton and Cow Roast where the inn serves good food and drinks and has a very pleasant garden.

The route: A short to medium length route on minor roads and off-road tracks with just one serious climb, an ideal first outing.

From the car park **turn R** following the Icknield Way and descend into Aldbury, passing the start of the Icknield Way Riders' Route on the left and the Stocks Hotel, golf and country club on the right. Arrive in the village by the popular Greyhound Inn and pond and go straight ahead at the crossroads. Pass the village shop, **keep L** with the road by the Valiant Trooper, then **bear R** to follow Newground Road.

After passing over the railway and canal, cross the A4251 at New Ground to take Hemp Lane briefly before **turning L** on Bottom House Lane, just before the flyover. Where the lane turns sharp right and passes under the A41, a good bridleway leads **to the L** past Tinkers Lodge to the Cow Roast Inn. Cross the road from the inn to visit the very attractive lock and marina.

Return by the same bridleway and follow the lane under the A41 to climb up to Wood Row, now following the Icknield Way Riders' Route. At the top of the climb **turn R** onto Wigginton Bottom. At the end of this road **turn R**, again following the Icknield Way Riders' Route which is now followed for several miles until descending into

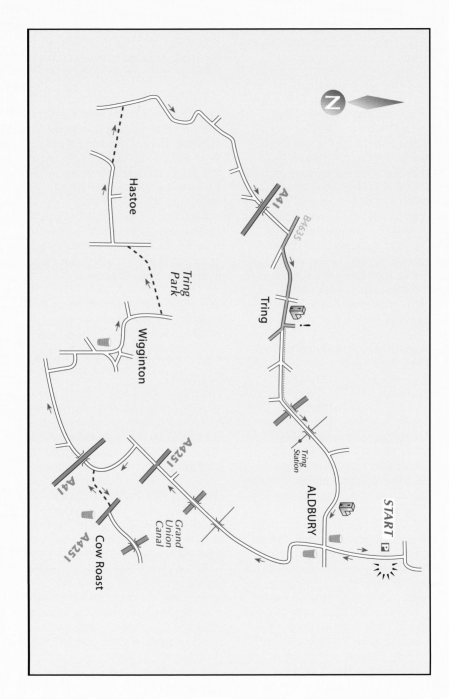

Tring. The route is waymarked either with specific signs or a flint axe symbol on normal bridleway signs, so look out for these.

Now pass the Greyhound pub in Wigginton before **turning L** at a four-way junction onto Vicarage Road. Follow this road for a further ½ mile, until after a sharp right-hand bend the road starts to descend. **Turn L** here onto the permissive bridleway above Tring Park, also signed for The Ridgeway; this turn is easy to miss. The off-road track is very good and even in winter presents little problem. The track follows a mainly level course through the woods with a small climb just before the exit to the road, and is easily distinguished from various footpaths and tracks leading off to the left and right.

After approximately 1 mile the track leads to a road where you **turn L**, and shortly **R** at a junction onto Church Lane signed for Hastoe. Follow the road through the village, **turning L** at the 'Give Way', and then at a sharp left-hand bend go straight on, following a bridleway which is the route of both the Icknield Way and The Ridgeway. In winter there can be a couple of muddy sections along here, but they are generally avoidable.

On emerging from the woods **turn R** and go downhill on the minor road where the bridleway and Icknield Way continue straight ahead. The route downhill is steep in places, so ensure your brakes are working. **Take care**, at the bottom of the steepest part of the hill there is a sharp right-hand bend. After a mile, **keep R** at the junction in Dancersend signed for Tring by a Buckland Parish notice board. Keep

with this road, ignoring lanes and byways to the right and after ¾ mile pass under the A41 to shortly arrive on the edge of Tring, where **turn R** at a T-junction with the Aylesbury road.

Go straight over a mini-roundabout onto the High Street and straight over the crossroads where the Zoological Museum is signed to the right. Pass the Rose and Crown Hotel on the right and the parish church of St Peter and St Paul on the left. Go straight across at a large roundabout and **bear L** signed for the station. A shared-use cycle path runs alongside Station Road which leads to the station after crossing once again the Grand Union canal on a left bend by a minor junction.

Pass the station, continuing on Station Road to Aldbury, there **turning L** to retrace your route to Pitstone Hill.

• •

ALDBURY
Aldbury village is an extremely popular spot for walkers and cyclists, particularly at weekends. This picturesque village with its 15th century inn, the Valiant Trooper, also features 600 year old stocks, a whipping post and a duck pond.

THE ICKNIELD WAY RIDERS' ROUTE
The section that is followed by our route, starting from Wood Row, forms part of a 23 mile off-road cycle route, that runs from Wain Hill near Bledlow, to Pitstone Hill car park. The Icknield Way itself is an ancient trading route that runs below the escarpment. The Riders' Route opened in 1998 for the use of walkers, cyclists and horse riders and follows mainly bridleways and quiet roads. A leaflet describing the route has been published by Buckinghamshire County Council and can be obtained from tourist information centres.

The picturesque village of Aldbury is a popular spot for cyclists

TRING ZOOLOGICAL MUSEUM

The Walter Rothschild Zoological Museum is to be found just off the route in the centre of Tring and is said to have the finest collection of stuffed mammals, birds, reptiles and insects in the country. It is open every day and has a picnic shelter, garden picnic area and a souvenir shop. Interestingly it is also available to hire for functions and receptions! It was Walter Rothschild who was also responsible for introducing the fat or edible dormouse into the area; apparently it was the Romans who earned this small rodent the title 'edible'.

Cholesbury, Chartridge and Chesham

10 miles

This is a ride on ancient lanes and ridge tops, clothed in beech woodland, in the central northern Chilterns. From Cholesbury the route passes through beautiful countryside, visiting the villages of St Leonards and Chartridge and following part of the ancient Grim's Ditch earthwork before skirting the edge of Chesham.

Map: OS Landranger 165 Aylesbury and Leighton Buzzard or OS Explorer 181 (GR 932071).

Starting point: Cholesbury is off the beaten track, the closest 'A' roads being the A416 through Chesham to the south-east and the A41 to the north near Tring. There is parking around the common. The route is described starting from a small car park by the cricket pavilion and bus stop at the west end of the common, and on the north side of the road.

By train: Chesham station is on a spur from Chalfont and Latimer on the London Underground Metropolitan line. From here the route can be joined on the Asheridge road by following the Chiltern Heritage Trail, Hampden Route out of Chesham.

Refreshments: There are no facilities at the start but the Full Moon pub is close by and is very popular and recommended for a drink on your return. Pubs on the route include the Bell, Chartridge, offering food, a garden and a warm welcome, and the Blue Ball, Asheridge.

The route: An easy circuit on mostly quiet lanes and so ideal with children, with the popular Cholesbury Common and Iron Age fort to explore on your return.

From the cricket pavilion **turn R** onto the road and immediately **R** again, signed for Wigginton and Tring. Shortly after the duck pond on the left, **turn L** onto Shire Lane.

Follow this lane for 1¼ miles through the woods, until reaching a private road on the left by a house and farm building on the right. **Turn L** onto this road, signed as a bridleway, but a good track throughout. This follows the line of Grim's Ditch and leads to a junction with another minor road by Leylands Farm. **Turn L** here and descend. On reaching the houses at the edge of St Leonards **turn R** to climb Gilbert's Hill to a junction. **Turn R**, signed for Wendover, and then shortly L, signed for The Lee and Great Missenden. Follow the road as it winds gently to a sharp right bend by a cottage, and then

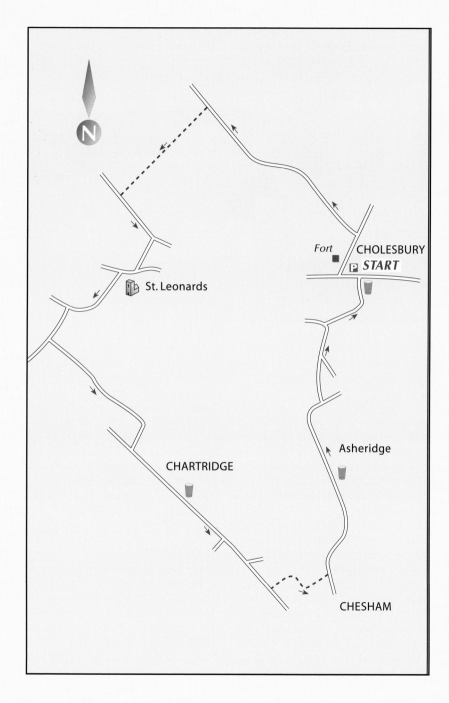

N

Fort

CHOLESBURY

P *START*

St. Leonards

Asheridge

CHARTRIDGE

CHESHAM

Along the Grim's Ditch: a pleasant place to do some repairs

a sharp left by a junction. At the top of a short climb **turn L** onto Arrewig Lane.

A long gradual descent, passing through Arrewig Farm, leads to a sharp right-hand bend. Climb then steeply to a junction with a more major road, **turn L** here heading for Chartridge. Pass the Conference Centre and the Bell on the left, followed by Westdean Lane on the right. After Old Sax Lane on the left, take the **next L** onto Buslins Lane, signed 'unsuitable for motors' and easily missed between the houses.

Descend steeply and then follow the rough track through to a road on the outskirts of Chesham. **Turn L** here and climb steeply and then more gradually into Asheridge village. Pass the Blue Ball public house, and after leaving the village follow the road **to the R** at a

small green near Asheridge Farm. **Turn L** by the junction with Bank Green.

Turn L at the next junction, and then **R** onto Ray's Hill by the pond, signed for Cholesbury. A descent followed by a steep climb then brings you back to Cholesbury Common by the Full Moon and windmill (hidden behind the houses to your right). **Turn L** here to arrive back at the parking.

• •

CHOLESBURY

To the west of Cholesbury Common, just across the road from our starting point, is Cholesbury Fort. This is an Iron Age structure covering 10 acres and housing the church of St Lawrence, which was rebuilt in 1872. The windmill is a brick tower mill that was built in 1884 and was operational until the First World War. It is now a private residence.

GRIM'S DITCH

Grim's Ditch is in fact a collective name used to describe several sets of linear earthworks found across the Chilterns with no origin or purpose in common. Although no conclusive evidence has been found to explain the existence of these structures, this particular one may have some relation to Cholesbury Fort and is thought to originate from the same period (Iron Age).

BEECH WOODLAND

On this ride, as with many in the Chilterns, beech woodland is strongly in evidence. These woods were planted and maintained to provide the raw materials of local industry, namely the supply of fuel wood and later for furniture making. Unlike modern day forest harvesting where trees are felled, the beech wood was taken in a manner that allowed the tree to provide successive crops. The two principal techniques for achieving this were pollarding and coppicing. In coppicing the tree is cut back to ground level from where new shoots spring up. This could be a problem in woodland that is also used for livestock grazing, as many woods were, as the animals would eat the new growth. In these cases pollarding would be employed, when the wood is cut back to around 8 feet from the ground, where new growth then occurs. Evidence of both methods can still be seen in the remaining woodlands, though the majority of current trees form a high canopy resulting in the typical thinly vegetated woodland floor of the Chilterns. The most successful coloniser of this niche, the bluebell, owes its success to flowering in spring, before the beech comes into leaf blocking the light from the woodland floor below.

Asheridge

Off-road in Wendover Woods

4 miles

A short ride in Forestry Commission woodland along designated off-road cycle trails. There is a network of such signed trails within Wendover Woods for the use of cyclists, horse riders and pedestrians alike (those trails usable by cyclists are clearly marked, the others should not be used) making this a great location in which to enjoy the Chiltern woodland and views – you can even plan a barbecue along the way! This route is a circuit of the wood using the majority of available trails, and is an ideal introduction to off-road cycling. Access arrangements do change, so if the route described here is marked as not for use by cyclists when you visit, please observe the signs and find an alternative.

Map: OS Landranger 165 Aylesbury and Leighton Buzzard or OS Explorer 181 (GR 889090). There is also a Forestry Commission sketch map showing cycle trails; this is ideal and you can usually get a copy from the local tourist information centre in Wendover.

Starting point: There is ample parking in the woods (pay and display). This is accessed from Aston Hill, off the A4011 Wendover to Tring road. Note that the road system within the woods is one-way and you will exit approximately 1 mile further along the road.

By train: Wendover is the nearest station, on the London Marylebone to Aylesbury line, from where the route is most easily joined from the cycle access point on Hale Lane.

Refreshments: There is a toilet block close to the car park, but no fixed refreshment sales. However, there is often a mobile ice cream van. There are barbecue points provided should you wish to take along food and cook alfresco, these can be booked by phoning the Forestry Commission office on 01296 625825, Monday, Wednesday or Friday between 9 am and 1 pm.

The route: The trails are generally in good condition all year, though a couple do have significant surface mud in winter. The tracks are wide and easy to ride but they are steep in places and so quite strenuous.

Once parked find the way to the start of the Orienteering Trail, which is also the start of the route. This can be found by following the main tarmac road past the main parking areas and toilet block, heading for the exit, and signed for the Orienteering Course. The track required is on the right, in sight

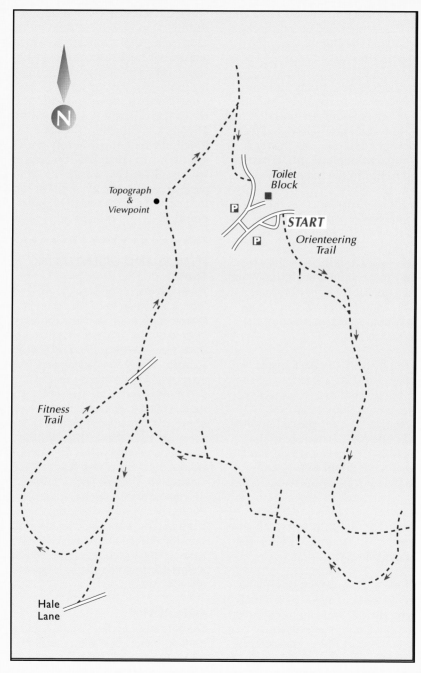

of the toilet block and marked as a bike trail, with a large wooden sign to the right marking the start of the Orienteering Trail.

Follow the trail descending and with impressive views to the right. As with many of the downhill sections, the trail is fast, so **watch your speed** and look out for other trail users. As the track levels out continue straight on passing a hairpin turn to the right.

The track now continues on the level for ½ mile before reaching a cross-junction, at which **turn R**, signed for the mountain bike trail. Descend now into the valley bottom. In winter this section can be slippery with some mud, so **take care**. In the valley bottom, cross the main track and start a long gradual climb to regain much of the height just lost.

From the bottom, the track bends first right then left. Pass a track to the right and continue climbing, passing a viewing point to the left on the Firecrest Trail. Shortly after a bird hide below to the right, and also on the Firecrest Trail, **turn sharp L** to climb a little way further, but more gently, before the track then descends.

(If you want a short cut, ignore this left turn and carry on until you reach a car turning circle. Continue with the last paragraph below.)

Follow the track downhill, this can be slippery in winter. On reaching a track to the right, **turn R**. This climbs gradually until levelling out to give extensive views over the Aylesbury Vale. Continue past a crossing with the fitness trail to arrive at the car turning circle, by the sign for Boddington Hill Fort.

Leave the track here and head across a short section of grass **to the L** of the car turning circle, to reach a barrier and a downhill track. Follow this to a fork, where **turn R**. The track then runs level for some way, passing an ideal spot for a break, with a topograph and views across the vale and to Coombe Hill. The track eventually arrives at a T-junction where **turn sharply R** and uphill. A stiff climb ends on tarmac, where a **R turn** leads back into the parking area, passing a signpost for the footpath to the Chilterns' highest point.

● ●

FITNESS AND ORIENTEERING TRAILS

There are many things to do in Wendover Woods including fixed Fitness and Orienteering trails, should a combination of exercises be required. The fitness trail starts from the car turning circle at the southern end of the parking area (passed on route). A fixed board provides information and marks the start of the route, which is circular, taking in a series of exercise stations complete with necessary equipment. There are also many orienteering points throughout the woods. Short posts with red markings indicate the checkpoints; with the designated start point being located at the top of the track where this cycle route begins. A specific orienteering map, showing checkpoint locations, terrain type etc and including suggested routes is available from the tourist information office in Wendover.

FIRECREST

This tiny and rare British bird is found living in these woodlands. A walking route, The Firecrest Trail, is named after it, and includes hides from where this elusive resident may be glimpsed.

The cycle trails in Wendover Woods are good all year round

Topograph and viewpoint looking towards Coombe Hill

ASTON HILL WOODS

Purpose-built cross country and downhill mountain bike trails are available just over the road in Aston Hill woods. Entry is restricted to members (for insurance purposes), though day membership is available. Aston Hill is not a place for beginners, but nor do you need to be an expert, once you have mastered the basics of off-road riding there will be something for you there.

The Misbourne Valley

17½ miles

A varied tour of the Misbourne valley and surrounding hills, taking in attractive villages such as Great and Little Missenden, The Lee and Holmer Green, with their brick and flint pubs, elegant coaching inns and delightful greens, along with intervening ubiquitous Chiltern beech woods.

Map: OS Landranger 165 Aylesbury and Leighton Buzzard or OS Explorer 181 and 172 (GR 894015).

Starting point: Start from Great Missenden Link Road car park, on the A4128 near its junction with the A413.

By train: The nearest station is Great Missenden on the London Marylebone to Aylesbury line.

Refreshments: There are several pubs and restaurants, and one small café on the main street in Great Missenden. There are also a supermarket and newsagent (both open on Sundays) near the station. Of the pubs the Cross Keys is recommended, offering good beer a warm welcome. Along the route there are frequent pubs, but few other amenities, though brief diversions into Chesham or Holmer Green give quick access to shops should you need them. The Crown in Little Missenden and the Full Moon in Little Kingshill, towards the end of the route, are recommended.

The route: The circuit is quite hilly so be prepared for a few stiff climbs, but the scenery makes it worthwhile.

From the car park **turn L** and then **R**, signed for the Memorial Hall car park, to join a shared-use footpath by the playing fields. Note that this path and other parts of the route coincide with the Mid Chiltern Villages Cycle Ride marked by blue cycleway signs with the number 3. Other parts of the route coincide with the Chiltern Heritage Trail, another signed cycle route.

The path emerges at a turning circle outside a school, where **turn L** and

pass the Chiltern Heritage Trail ceramic plaque to follow another shared-use path through two underpasses. Alternatively, if a visit to the parish church of Great Missenden, now stranded from the village by the bypass, is desired **turn R** at the turning circle onto the lane leading into Great Missenden, and then, almost immediately, **L** by a horse trough. Follow this lane over the bypass to the church, and then return to follow the aforementioned path.

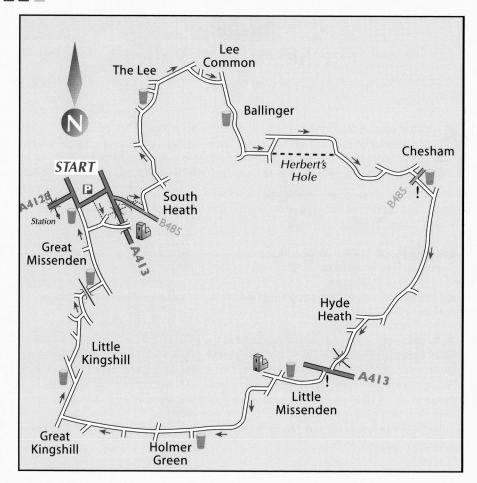

After the second underpass **turn R** after some steps to follow a short access road uphill to a cycle lane. This leads to a junction, where **turn steeply L** onto Frith Hill, South Heath leg.

Frith Hill then leads into South Heath, where take the **first L** at a crossroads onto Potter Row, signed for The Lee. After just over a mile, and after passing Leather Lane on the left, this leads to a junction on a sharp right bend in Hunts Green. Continue with the main road, soon passing the incongruous Earl Howe figurehead before arriving at the Cock

and Rabbit public house in The Lee.

Pass the pub and common and **turn R** by the cross, heading for Lee Common. Follow this road until just after passing a Scout Centre, **turn R** onto Oxford Street and continue through Lee Common, passing an ornate well on the left, to reach a T-junction where **turn R** for Ballinger.

Follow this road as it descends steeply into Ballinger Bottom, and then climbs out to Ballinger Common, passing the Pheasant on the right, before again

This Chiltern Heritage Trail ceramic plaque can be seen en route

descending into Ballinger Bottom South. **Turn L** when the main road bends sharply to the right. Continue downhill to a fork by Herbert's Hole Cottage. **Turn L** here and go steeply uphill, to a T-junction where **turn R** for Little Pednor.

Pass through the delightful courtyard at Little Pednor and then along the ridge for some way, before descending into the valley shortly after the Chesham boundary sign. After the valley bottom the road then climbs briefly before another drop to a T-junction, where you **turn R**.

On entering the built up area of Chesham, and just past a tennis club, **turn R** on Pednormead End to the Queen's Head. **Turn R** and then immediately **L** by the pub and over the nascent River Chess. **Take care here** as the road can be busy and visibility is poor at the junction. Take the **second R** onto Fuller's Hill, to climb out of the valley, passing Fuller's Hill Farm and White House Farm towards the top of the hill. Ignore a left turn for Amersham, and follow the road round to the right into Hyde Heath, where take the **first L** onto Keepers Lane. Where the road bears right, **turn L** to keep on Keepers Lane, which then descends, crossing the railway to the busy A413.

Turn R at the bottom of Keepers Lane onto the small access road, not onto the dual carriageway. This leads to a better crossing point, where cross to the minor road leading to Little Missenden. Visibility is good at this point, and the central refuge makes crossing safe, but still **take care** – speeding vehicles are common on this road.

Follow the road into Little Missenden, and pass the Crown and Red Lion public houses before **turning L** towards Holmer Green just before the church. Keep with this lane as it twists and turns, and dips and climbs to eventually arrive at Holmer Green and the Bat and Ball public house. Continue straight ahead, passing the common to arrive at a double mini-roundabout by the Mandarin Duck Chinese restaurant. Go straight on here, for just over 1 mile to a 'Give Way' at a T-junction in Great Kingshill. **Turn R** here and shortly arrive in Little Kingshill, where **turn L** by the Prince of Wales.

Pass the Full Moon and continue along Hare Lane, ignoring private New Road to the left. On reaching Longfield **turn R** to keep on Hare Lane, and descend steeply to a junction. **Turn R** and then **L** here, to rejoin the main road and continue downhill briefly, before passing under the railway bridge and then **turning L** by the Nag's Head. This road leads back into Great Missenden, by the traffic-calmed High Street, which in turn leads to the Link Road and railway station.

THE EARL HOWE FIGUREHEAD

Standing at the entrance of Pipers, this colourful ship's figurehead comes as quite a shock on cycling towards The Lee. The figurehead of Admiral Earl Howe comes from the *Howe*, the last of the British Navy's wooden warships. When this ship was broken up early last century (1920s) the timbers were purchased by local businessman Arthur Liberty and used in building Liberty's of Regent Street. The figurehead was evidently kept as a memento and oversized garden ornament!

GREAT MISSENDEN

The village at the start of the route most probably owes its existence to the spring at Mobwell, just to the north, and the source of the River Misbourne. Ancient settlement in the Chilterns took place mainly along the foot of the escarpment, which coincided with the Icknield Way – then the major communication route in the area, long before radial routes from London came to dominate. When settlement moved into the heart of the Chilterns, most likely in Anglo-Saxon times, water supply was a key factor in these chalk hills. Although today the flow of the River Misbourne has been greatly reduced by over use, in the past it would have been a much more reliable source, and sufficient to supply the growth of the new settlements in the valley. The later history of Missenden has been strongly influenced by the change in orientation of the major trade routes mentioned above. Firstly it became an important coach stop, as evidenced by the remaining coaching inns in the high street, and then later, a stop on the new Metropolitan Railway, when its current London dormitory function began to be established. Through this later stage it has still managed to retain individuality sadly lost in much of 'metro land'.

THE CHILTERN HERITAGE CYCLING TRAILS

A feature of the Chiltern Heritage Cycling Trails, opened in 2000, is the specially commissioned artwork. This includes a colourful ceramic plaque on the wall outside Great Missenden School on an educational theme, and at a junction in Little Missenden, a carved wooden totem pole pointing the way.

The decorative signpost in Little Missenden

10

Black Park and Hedgerley

14½ miles

Despite running so close to one of the country's busiest motorways, this route finds contrastingly quiet lanes. The start in Black Park is a great cycling location especially with young children, and well worth a visit in its own right. Skirting the famous Pinewood Studios, the ride heads for Gerrards Cross, before taking quieter country roads back towards Stoke Poges, with a stop at an idyllic country inn.

Map: OS Landranger 176 West London or OS Explorer 172 (GR 005832).

Starting point: There is good car parking (fee payable) at the start in Black Park Country Park, signed from the A412 Uxbridge to Slough road.

By train: The nearest station is Gerrards Cross on the London Marylebone, High Wycombe, Aylesbury line, about 1 mile north of the route. The route is most easily joined by following the B416 south from Gerrards Cross, crossing Gerrards Cross Common and the A40 to the end of Hedgerley Lane.

Refreshments: There are refreshments and toilets in the park by the lake. Several pubs are passed en route, the White Horse at Hedgerley being strongly recommended.

The route: Cycling is permitted throughout most of Black Park, though some paths are marked as 'no cycling' – please observe these so as not to jeopardise future cycling access. The route described uses paths on which cycling is permitted to reach the bridleway running along the east of the park. Future changes could mean that cycling is not permitted on the route described – if this happens please walk and push your bike, or follow an alternate route to the bridleway.

Enter Black Park by the main gate, opposite the car park entrance and at the far end of the car park. This leads to a complex junction, where **bear R** to follow a tarmac path around the head of the lake. This path ends at the edge of an open piece of ground, where follow the gravel track to the right, and along the edge of the open ground. Keep in this general direction for ¼ mile, to a cross-junction in the woods, where turn left, signed as a footpath and the Beeches Way.

On reaching an exit onto the A412, **turn L** to join a bridleway that runs along the eastern edge of the park. The actual bridleway is parallel and adjacent to the right of the track being followed, separated from it by a low

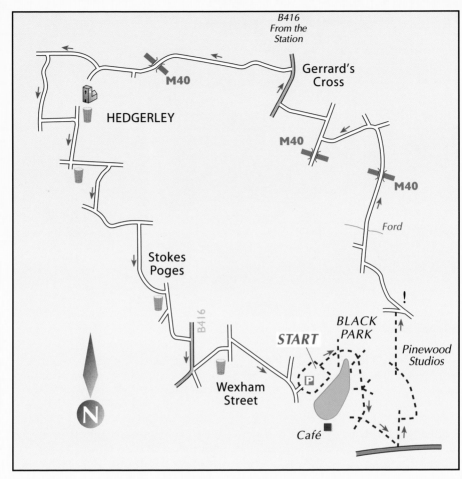

fence. After 200 yards the bridleway turns to the right, and a gate in the fence allows access from the track being followed. After passing a gate into Pinewood Studios on the right, **keep R** at a junction to maintain the same direction along the edge of the wood.

Leave the wood by the exit at the end of the bridleway, and cross the road to join Alderbourne Lane by the entrance to Alderbourne Farm; **take care** as the exit from the woods is on a bend in the

road. Descend, passing Cherry Tree Lane to the left, and where Alderbourne Lane continues to the left, go straight ahead and through the ford (check the depth first!).

Climb and then cross the M40 bridge, and at a junction on a left bend, **turn L** heading for Fulmer. At the end of Fulmer Lane **turn R** and climb towards Gerrards Cross. Just after passing the Gerrards Cross sign and a traffic flow restriction **turn L** onto the residential Fulmer Drive. Where this road meets

The ford at Alderbourne

the B416 **turn R** and just after a left-hand bend, **turn L** onto Hedgerley Lane.

Shortly after re-crossing the M40, **turn R** to remain on Hedgerley Lane as the main road continues as Village Lane down into Hedgerley. As the road dips, just after passing the Junction 2 sign to the right on the motorway, **turn L** onto a small lane through woodland. After a descent **turn L** onto Kiln Lane which leads into Hedgerley. At the T-junction **turn L** to visit the White Horse, otherwise **turn R** and climb to Hedgerley Hill and **turn L** at a 'Give Way' by the One Pin Inn. Take the **first R** in approximately 300 yards onto a small lane through the woods. **Turn L** at the end of the lane and at a row of houses on the left, **turn R** into Duffield Lane.

Turn **R** at the end of the lane by the Dog and Pot, and **L** at a fork onto Rogers Lane. At the 'Give Way' with Bell's Hill, **turn R** and shortly **L** onto Farthing Green Lane. At the end of this lane **turn L** and then almost immediately **R** onto Rowley Lane, signed for Iver Heath. This leads back to the car park, on the left just after passing Black Park Road.

BLACK PARK

The Park is a large recreational area covering around 500 acres of mixed woodland, with nature trails, bridleways and even routes for horse-drawn carriages!

PINEWOOD FILM STUDIOS

This route runs close by Pinewood Film Studios, home of the famous Carry On films. The studios are situated in the 90

Black Park

acres that surround the stately home of Heatherden Hall, originally a country club belonging to Charles Boot of 'Boots the Chemist'. During the heyday of the 1950s Pinewood were making 20 to 30 films per year.

CHERRY ORCHARDS

Cherry Tree Lane is a reminder of the number of cherry orchards that were common in this region in the past, being a key element of the local economy. There are still cherry trees to be seen and they are particularly attractive when in blossom in the spring.

THE CHILTERN SOCIETY

The planning of the M40 motorway also saw the foundations of the Chiltern Society, as a group of people got together to try and prevent this road cutting through the Chilterns. The M40 itself for all its flaws has at least concentrated traffic away from Chiltern lanes, as seen on this route. Although this mission failed, the Chiltern Society has gone from strength to strength as a local group that cares about its environment and actively works to maintain the unique character of the Chiltern Hills.

11
Whiteleaf Hill and Chequers

14 miles

A circuit of Chiltern hilltop lanes around the Prime Minister's country retreat, setting out from the impressive and popular viewpoint of Whiteleaf Hill. Besides the exceptional views, this is also a route with interesting political connections, passing as it does not only Chequers but also the Hampdens, picturesque villages with their connection to John Hampden, the patriot, of Civil War fame. The ride also passes a Neolithic burial chamber, a 17th century smock mill at Lacey Green, and a working pottery at Speen.

Map: OS Landranger 165 Aylesbury and Leighton Buzzard or OS Explorer 181 and 172 (GR 823036).

Starting point: There is a small car park and picnic site at Whiteleaf Hill, but no facilities. The start is most easily approached from Monks Risborough via the minor road passing Whiteleaf village and climbing steeply up the hill.

By train: Princes Risborough station is on the London Marylebone to Birmingham via High Wycombe line, and Monks Risborough is on a spur of this line to Aylesbury. Both stations are close to the route where it passes through Whiteleaf.

Refreshments: There are ample opportunities for pub stops on the route, ones of note being the Red Lion, Whiteleaf (but rather early in the route!), the Hampden Arms, Great Hampden (although all tables are generally reserved for diners, there is a good garden for fine days), the Whip, Lacey Green (pretty garden with excellent views of the Lacey Green windmill), and the Pink and Lily, Parslows Hillock. While passing through Great Kimble it is also worth stopping at the Bernard Arms to see the memorabilia of visits by Prime Ministers and other world leaders, a consequence of its proximity to Chequers.

The route: A hilly route on minor roads, some of the climbs would be testing for beginners, but you can always push.

Before setting off, a brief diversion to the Whiteleaf Hill viewpoint is recommended – it is only a few hundred yards from the car park. To reach it follow the track past the information boards and **turn R** on the bridleway. This very quickly brings you to a gate that opens onto the summit

of the hill, with the ancient long barrow to the left. Once you have savoured the views return by the bridleway to start the route proper.

Turn R and proceed downhill where the bridleway meets the road. **Take care** descending this steep hill, and be

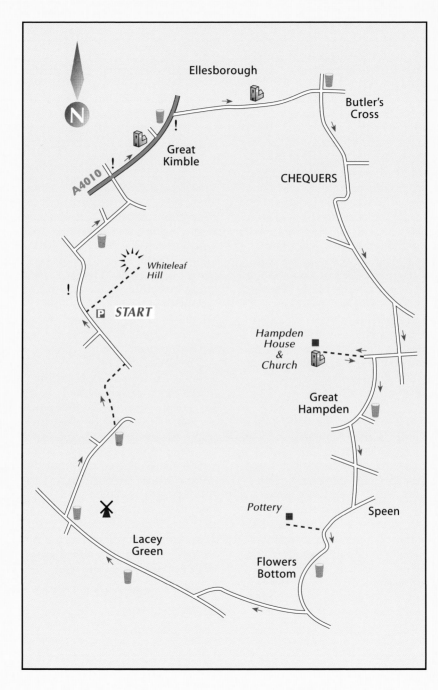

Ellesborough

Butler's
Cross

Great
Kimble

A4010

CHEQUERS

Whiteleaf
Hill

START

Hampden
House
&
Church

Great
Hampden

Pottery

Speen

Lacey
Green

Flowers
Bottom

careful not to miss the **R turn** into Whiteleaf village, directly opposite the Icknield Way on the left. This road leads through the village, past the Red Lion, and to a 'Give Way' at a T-junction with the Cadsden road, where you **turn L**. At the roundabout junction with the A4010 **turn R**.

Follow the busy 'A' road for approximately 1 mile, passing the Bernard Arms on your left, before **turning R with care** in Little Kimble heading for Wendover on Ellesborough Road. Note the views to the slopes of Cymbeline's Castle on your right. After passing through Ellesborough, the junction of Butler's Cross is reached below the monument of Coombe Hill. **Turn R** here and start a long climb that gradually steepens to arrive at a junction by an entrance to Chequers. Continue straight on and keep with this road for almost 2 miles, passing one junction to the right, before reaching Hampden Bottom Farm, shortly after which **turn R**.

Climb to a crossroads and there **turn R**, and follow the road through a sharp left bend to Great Hampden. The track that continues straight on at this bend leads to Hampden House and church, and is a bridleway, which offers a recommended diversion. The bridleway can be followed all the way back to Whiteleaf Hill, and in summer this provides an interesting mountain bike route.

In Great Hampden ignore the left turn just after the Hampden Arms, but take the **next L** heading for Speen. Continue straight ahead at a cross-junction with another minor road to eventually arrive in Speen. Pass the King William restaurant to **turn R** at a T-junction by Speen Stores. Descend

steeply into Flowers Bottom, via a left-hand hairpin bend, where a track to the right leads off to Speen Pottery.

An equally steep climb then leads out of Flowers Bottom, passing the Plough Bistro, to arrive at a junction by the 'Home of Rest for Horses' where Slad Lane is taken **to the R**. This leads to a T-junction with a more major road; **turn R** into Lacey Green.

After passing through Lacey Green, and before a steep descent, **turn R** by the Whip public house and the close-by restored windmill. Follow Pink Road, with occasional good views to the left, and passing the Widmer Feeds pet centre on the right. Widmer Feeds sells almost everything you could think of to do with animals. It has a little animal park that the children will enjoy looking around; there is a small entrance charge.

Arrive at Parslows Hillock and the Pink and Lily public house with its Rupert Brooke connections. Shortly beyond the pub, at a sharp right bend, **turn L** onto a bridleway which soon enters woodland to the right. A good off-road track is then followed for ¾ mile before **turning L** onto the road leading back to Whiteleaf Hill. There are a couple of muddy patches towards the end of this bridleway in winter, nothing much, but these can be avoided by staying with the road, turning left and left again to arrive at the same point.

● ●

WHITELEAF HILL

The long barrow, which is seen at the beginning of our route, is of Neolithic date, and was found to contain the body of a man in a wooden burial chamber when it was excavated between 1935

The sign at Great Kimble commemorating John Hampden

Warm autumn colour along the bridleway at Whiteleaf Hill

and 1939. Cut into the hillside below this is Whiteleaf Cross, which is thought possibly to be the work of medieval monks from Monks Risborough or Missenden Abbey.

LACEY GREEN WINDMILL
Dating from the mid 17th century, this is thought to be the oldest surviving smock mill in England. It was brought to its present site from Chesham in 1821. Between 1972 and 1978 the Chiltern Society worked on its restoration and the mill is now open to the public on summer Sunday afternoons.

SPEEN POTTERY
Speen Pottery is one of those wonderful cottage industries that can still occasionally be found. The potter lives and works on the site, moulding and firing her pieces to be eventually

decorated in her own unique style. You may be lucky enough to be able to see the work in progress.

CHEQUERS
Chequers was given to the Nation in 1917 by Lord Lee of Fareham as a country residence for the British Prime Minister. The thinking behind this was that 'fresh air and fine views might lead to sound judgement'. Public footpaths cross parts of the Chequers estate, but the 16th century house itself is closed to the public.

COOMBE HILL
Coombe Hill near Princes Risborough is one of the highest points in the Chilterns at 857 feet. The monument at the summit was erected in 1901 in memory of the many soldiers killed in the Boer War.

Beaconsfield and Penn

11 miles

Quaker connections and a chance to visit the popular Bekonscot model village in the heart of 'Metro-land' at Beaconsfield enhance this ride. The route leads to Seer Green and then north to Coleshill, before returning past Hertfordshire House and through Penn village.

Map: OS Landranger 175 Reading and Windsor (and a tiny bit on 165 Aylesbury and Leighton Buzzard) or OS Explorer 172 (GR 940911).

Starting point: The A40 passes through the old town of Beaconsfield, and the B474 leaves the 'A' road at a roundabout by the church heading for the new town. There is on-road parking by the A40 in the old town, and there are car parks by the station and model village in the new. The route is described starting at the rail station, so wherever you park make your way there, or join the route at an appropriate point.

By train: Beaconsfield station is on the London Marylebone – High Wycombe – Aylesbury and Birmingham line.

Refreshments: Beaconsfield, like Amersham, which also developed along the Metropolitan railway, has an old town and a new town built up around the railway station. The old town has the pubs and restaurants, the new, the shops and the model village.

The route: Another route sharing parts of the Chiltern Heritage Cycling Trails, this time the ride uses the Southern Way or Milton Loop, including a very pleasant off-road section through Hodgemoor Woods. Never far from major centres of population, this route still manages to find secluded corners, and give a feeling of being away from it all.

From the station cycle up the road away from the car park (rail users only) and **turn R** at the top. Go straight across at the large roundabout by Waitrose, then **first R** signed for parking. Pass Warwick Road car park and then Bekonscot model village on the left. At the end of the road, **turn L** in front of the church onto Grenfell Road. Follow the road round to the

right and then **turn L** onto Wilton Road, then **R** to meet the main road, then **turn R** again.

At the next junction, **turn L** onto the busy Amersham road, and **directly R with care** onto Longbottom Lane heading for Jordans and Seer Green. Take the **first L** off Longbottom Lane onto Bottom Lane and where the road

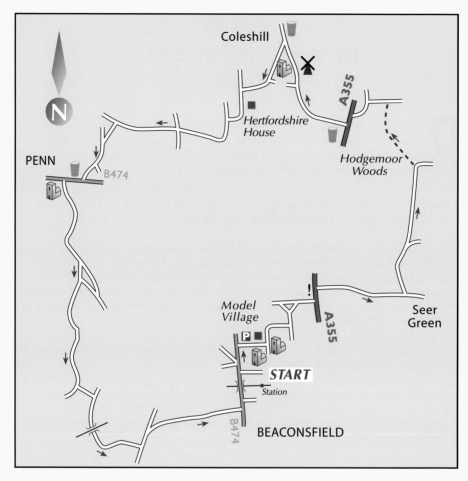

bears right and becomes Orchard Road, follow the single-track road to stay on Bottom Lane.

As the road bends sharp right by the gated entrance to a wood, continue into the wood and **turn L** to follow the bridleway. This is part of the Chiltern Heritage Trail, Milton Loop. Follow the blue posts through the woods; this bridleway can have a few muddy patches, but is generally good.

Eventually the bridleway leads to a road, where **turn L** and descend the hill. At the bottom of the hill **turn L** to join the cycleway alongside the busy 'A' road. Opposite the Magpies pub, cross the road using the new cycleway to gain access to Magpies Lane on the right. Climb Magpies Lane towards Coleshill, and **bear R** at a junction to continue climbing towards the village centre, passing the windmill on the right and common on the left.

Pass the Red Lion public house, opposite the large village pond, and by the church turn **sharp L** to almost double back on yourself. Continue

The Magpies, Magpie Lane, Coleshill

straight on at the junction with Chalk Hill and at the sharp right-hand bend by the Winchmore Hill sign **turn L.** Continue downhill passing the impressive Hertfordshire House on the left and at the T-junction **turn L. Bear R** at the bottom of the hill, and at the crossroads go straight ahead signed for Hazlemere.

Take the **first** L onto a minor lane just before Penn House Farm. Climb to a fork and **bear R** to meet the busy B474. **Turn R with care** and then shortly L onto Paul's Hill by the church and with the Crown public house on the right. This is a minor lane but is used by traffic so **take care** on the bends while descending. At a fork by a small wood **turn R. Keep R** where a small lane joins from the left, to contour along the hillside. After the lane turns sharp left and descends more steeply take the minor lane **on the L** where the road continues sharp right and upwards.

Descend to a junction with Riding Lane and **turn R.** This rough track leads under the railway and back to a road where **turn L.** Keep with the road bearing sharp right to climb back to Beaconsfield and **turn L** at the mini-roundabout to return to the start of the route.

● ●

BEKONSCOT

Bekonscot Model Village portrays rural England in the 1930s and is the oldest model village in the world. It includes numerous moving models amongst its six villages each with their own miniature population. A spectacular Gauge 1 model railway runs throughout the 1½ acre site. Bekonscot is open daily from mid February till the end of October and offers a picnic area, refreshment kiosk and souvenir shop.

HERTFORDSHIRE HOUSE

Hertfordshire House recalls a time when Coleshill was a detached island of Hertfordshire embedded in Buckinghamshire. Thomas Ellwood who owned the house made use of this fact to hold illegal Quaker meetings, being too remote for the Hertfordshire magistrates to concern themselves with.

WILLIAM PENN

William Penn, founder of Pennsylvania, was buried in 1718 alongside his two wives and their children in the grounds of the Friends' Meeting House at Jordans (just off this route). This Quaker meeting house was built in 1688 and is still in regular use. The village of Penn, named from the old word for a hill or headland, is often linked with William Penn, but no connection has been proven.

Hughenden Manor and Downley Common

2½ miles

A short, almost traffic free, and mostly off-road ride, around the former home of Disraeli, leaving plenty of time to see this popular National Trust property. An ideal introduction to off-road cycling, this route takes the bridleway that passes through the estate to Downley, circles the common and then returns by the same route.

Map: OS Landranger 165 Aylesbury and Leighton Buzzard or OS Explorer 172 (GR 861955).

Starting point: Hughenden Manor is reached from the A4128 High Wycombe to Missenden road. There is ample car parking at the top of the hill beyond the church. The car park is open from 8 am to 6 pm.

By train: High Wycombe station is on the London Marylebone to Birmingham and Aylesbury line. As the Manor is only a short distance from High Wycombe, using the train and cycling from and to High Wycombe station would be feasible, although this includes a rather busy road.

Refreshments: Hidden along a track in Downley is a delightful pub with a good garden, the Le De Spencer Arms, which makes an ideal break point along the route.

The route: Being only a little over 2 miles in distance, this is a perfect ride for novice off-road cyclists and children.

From the main car park head towards the buildings, passing an information board and a picnic area on the right. This leads past another small car park, complete with cycle parking, and shortly to the road by the manor. **Turn R** here, passing the manor on the left, to soon reach a bridleway on which descend through woodland; **take care** on the initial steep drop at the start of the bridleway.

The track then continues between open fields, passing a permitted bridleway to the right, before again entering woodland. Approximately ¼ mile into this wood a five-way footpath and bridleway junction by a National Trust sign is reached. The junction is marked by a finger post signing four of the directions, but not the bridleway **to the R**, which is the one to take. Climb quite steeply, **keeping L** where a

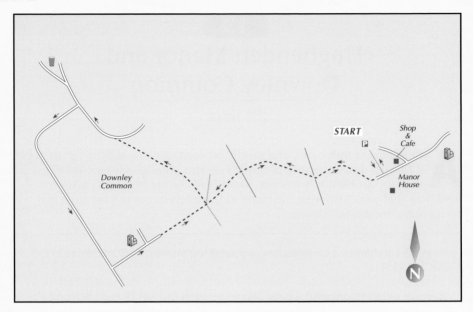

footpath forks to the right, to meet a gravel track by a row of houses along the east edge of the common.

Turn L onto the track, to shortly arrive at a junction with a tarmac road. If a break at the pub is desired, continue straight on here, and ignore a track to the right, to reach the Le De Spencer Arms.

Otherwise, **turn L** and follow the minor road around the common, and into a small valley. In the bottom of which, **turn L** onto Moor Lane. This left turn is very sharp and is hidden on the descent, so take care not to miss it. Where the lane ends at a chapel and small car park, continue straight ahead on the bridleway into the woods. This leads back to the five-way junction visited on the outward journey, continue straight ahead here to return to the Manor by the same route travelled earlier.

HUGHENDEN MANOR

Hughenden Manor, originally the home of Queen Victoria's favourite Prime Minister, Benjamin Disraeli, from 1848 until his death in 1881, is now in the hands of the National Trust. Many of the original pieces of furniture, pictures and books can still be seen in the house, which is open to the public along with the gardens at selected times. The surrounding park and woodlands provide beautiful walks all year round. A Victorian-themed, fully licensed stable yard restaurant is open at the same times as the house. There is also a visitor centre and gift shop in the adjacent courtyard. There are many footpaths around the estate that you may wish to explore following your ride – but remember no cycling on footpaths. In spring the bluebells in these woods are a spectacular sight.

The 14th century church of St Michael, Hughenden

HUGHENDEN CHURCHYARD

Hughenden churchyard provides the final resting-place for Disraeli and his wife, Mary Anne. The church of St Michael is 14th century and was remodelled between 1874 and 1890 by Sir Arthur Bloomfield. It also houses a monument to Disraeli erected near his usual pew in 1882 at the request of Queen Victoria.

THE GREEN WOODPECKER

The sound of the green woodpecker is common here, and generally among the woods and lanes of the Chilterns. Listen out for the loud and raucous cry that gives this bird its country name of 'yaffle', after which it may be spotted in low swooping flight as it moves from tree to tree.

14

Chinnor Hill and West Wycombe

15½ miles

Peaceful lanes and panoramic views with a visit to the largely National Trust-owned village of West Wycombe are offered on this ride. West Wycombe has many attractions, including its connection with the notorious Hell Fire Club, and is well worth spending a little time exploring before heading for Radnage and the heart of red kite country. Here on many days you'll see more of these splendid birds than you will cars. Chinnor Hill Nature Reserve, with its magnificent views across the Vale, rounds off the attractions before the route descends from Bledlow Ridge.

Map: OS Landranger 165 and 175 (very small section) or OS Explorer 171 and 172 (GR 813981).

Starting point: The route is described starting from Saunderton railway station, there is free parking close to the station if coming by car. The route could also be started from either West Wycombe, or Chinnor Hill Nature Reserve, both of which have parking, but West Wycombe can be very busy and parking at Chinnor Hill is limited, so Saunderton is preferred.

By train: Saunderton station is on the London Marylebone to Birmingham and Aylesbury via High Wycombe line.

Refreshments: There is a pub on the A4010 in Saunderton, but no other facilities – the station is un-manned. There are cafés, pubs and shops in West Wycombe, but the recommended stop is the Three Horseshoes in Bennett End. This is a classic country pub in a setting that is hard to beat, where you can sit and admire the views from the garden in the company of red kites circling overhead.

The route: A ride on surprisingly quiet lanes so close to the honeypot of West Wycombe and the busy roads leading into High Wycombe, with a few stiff climbs.

From the railway station **turn R**, climb through a sharp left bend and then descend into Slough Bottom. Keep with Slough Lane, ignoring Deanfield to the right and follow the valley bottom to a junction where **turn L** signed for High Wycombe.

On entering West Wycombe, and just before the main road, **turn L** onto West Wycombe Hill Road. A stiff climb leads past the Hell Fire Caves and café, and on to the National Trust-owned West Wycombe Hill. There are good views here and a gate at the top right of the car park gives access to the

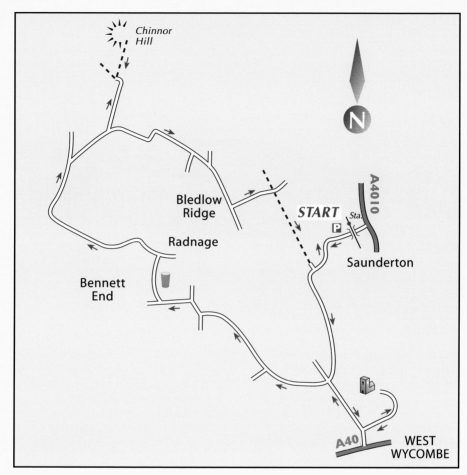

Dashwood Mausoleum and West Wycombe church, with its famous golden ball.

After exploring, return down the hill and **turn R** to return to the junction with Slough Lane. **Turn L** here onto Bottom Road, signed for Radnage. Pass Hatch Lane on the left, and continue heading for Bennett End and Town End. The road undulates up the valley, to a short steeper climb – with good views from the top – before descending to a junction and 'Give Way' sign.

Turn R signed for Town End, and almost immediately at the next junction **turn L**. This leads into Bennett End where **bear R** with the road at a junction and climb to the Three Horseshoes on the right.

After passing the pub the road levels and then descends to a junction, where **turn L**, pass Churchfield Farm and climb quite steeply out onto the ridge top by Andridge House and Farm. Pass the Sir Charles Napier Restaurant on the left, and after a sharp right bend

West Wycombe Hill, church and the Dashwood Mausoleum

and descent, **turn R** at a junction signed for Bledlow Ridge and High Wycombe to climb again briefly.

At the next sharp right bend, **turn L** onto Hill Top Lane to visit Chinnor Hill Nature Reserve. **Turn L** in front of the Nature Reserve sign in the small parking area, and then immediately **R** onto a bridleway. Follow this as far as a point where the woodland opens out onto grassland with views out over Chinnor and beyond, before retracing the route back to the car park.

Return by Hill Top Lane to the main road and **turn L** onto Red Lane which is followed into Bledlow Ridge. Ignore left and right turns, until after passing the church and a small petrol station on the left, and the post office to the right, take a **L turn** signed for Saunderton and Princes Risborough on Haw Lane.

Descend, and at the bottom of the hill, after a sharp right bend, **turn R** onto a bridleway before the road climbs again. This is a good track throughout, and leads back to Slough Lane. **Turn L** here to return to Saunderton station.

● ●

WEST WYCOMBE

West Wycombe village became the responsibility of the National Trust in 1933 and is made up of buildings which span several hundred years. On top of the hill the church is found within a 5th century Iron Age fort. The famous Golden Ball was added onto the tower in 1751 and provides seating for ten people, rumoured to be used as a drinking venue by the infamous Hell Fire Club! This was a society founded by Sir Francis Dashwood in the 1750s supposedly with religious connections, made up of men of wealth and influence and known for their bad behaviour.

Approaching Bennett End (photo courtesy of Nick Calkin)

Also found at the top of the hill is the Dashwood Mausoleum. Built in 1765 out of Portland stone and flint it provides the final resting-place for the Dashwood family.

The Caves were excavated on the site of a quarry in the 1750s to provide chalk foundations for the building of the road between West Wycombe and High Wycombe. They comprise a long series of tunnels that extend over ½ mile underground and are said to have played host to Chapter meetings of the afore-mentioned Hell Fire Club.

The church, Golden Ball Tower and Caves are open to visitors, mainly on summer afternoons. For details of visiting West Wycombe Park, house and grounds, contact the National Trust.

High Wycombe to the Thames Valley

12 miles

High Wycombe is not the most beautiful of towns it has to be said, but it does have a colourful past and many hidden treasures. It is also, of course, surrounded by delightful Chiltern countryside. Our route leaves town by the Wycombe 'east-west' cycleway and the popular Rye playing fields, before climbing out of the Wye Valley and descending into the Thames Valley to another cycleway. This leads via a couple of excellent lunch stop options, including one on a delightful stretch of the River Thames, to a gentler climb on quiet lanes back out of the valley, and an off-road descent back to the Rye.

Map: OS Landranger 175 Reading and Windsor or OS Explorer 172 (GR 870930).

Starting point: Plenty of parking is available in Wycombe, though it is busy on Saturdays. The route is described starting from the railway station, and passes through the car park at Railway Place.

By train: The nearest station is at High Wycombe, but the route also passes close to Bourne End on the Maidenhead to Marlow line.

Refreshments: High Wycombe is a medium sized town with many pubs, restaurants and shops. Several pubs and shops are passed en route. Worthy of note – and approximately half way – are the Spade Oak on the Thames near Well End, and the Queen's Head and King's Head in Little Marlow – all being very popular.

The route: A relatively short, but very varied route. Although there is one off-road section, the condition is generally good all year.

On leaving the station forecourt **turn L**, and just before the pedestrian crossing, directly opposite Castle Street on the right, **turn L** onto the path of Birdcage Walk. This is footpath only so it will be necessary to push on this section. This leads to a small road. Follow this a short distance and **turn first R** by the Irish Club into Railway Place car park.

Pass through the car park to the main road, and cross by the pedestrian crossing to enter the Rye by the restored Pann Mill. Cross the bridge, and **turn R**, continuing to meet the Wycombe cycleway at the edge of the Rye, where **turn L**, signed as a cycle route to Loudwater.

The route shortly arrives at a refreshment hut by a boating lake. Here the cycleway continues behind the lake, and is well marked on the

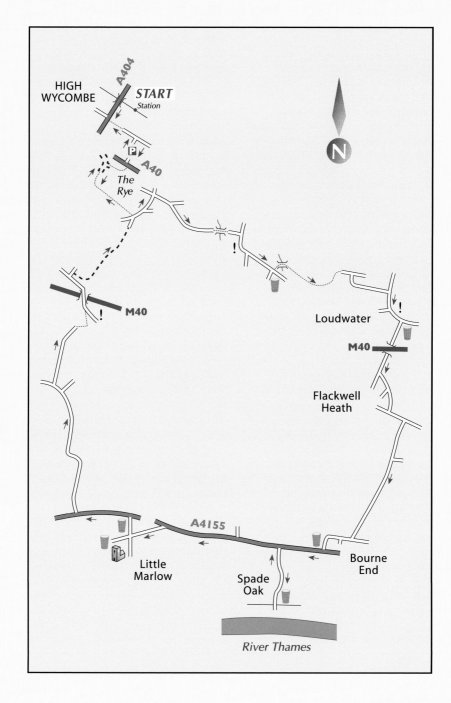

HIGH
WYCOMBE

A404

START
Station

P

A40

*The
Rye*

M40

N

Loudwater

M40

Flackwell
Heath

A4155

Little
Marlow

Spade
Oak

Bourne
End

River Thames

ground for its ¾ mile course in woodland behind the Rye.

Where the cycle path emerges on a minor road, **turn L** and follow this road downhill to a junction. **Turn R** here and wind through surprisingly pleasant and rural housing until reaching a bridge across a small stream. The bridge is quite narrow, so take care and be sure to give way to pedestrians.

A minor road then leads to a junction with a busier road at a sharp bend. **Turn R** here **with care**, ignore Abbey Barn Lane immediately to the right and continue to follow the cycleway signs along Kingsmead Road. Shortly after passing Spring Lane and the General Havelock pub on the right, **turn L** immediately before a traffic flow constriction, and re-cross Back Stream by another narrow bridge to enter King's Mead.

Follow the cycleway through the playing fields, ignoring opportunities to rejoin the road running in parallel to the right. After a car park, the cycle path becomes enclosed and leads to the residential Norwood Road. Shortly after joining this road **turn R** and join Fassets Road. This leads to the busy Station Road, **turn R** here to a mini-roundabout where **turn R** again to climb steeply up Treadaway Hill, heading for Flackwell Heath. A path follows alongside the hill, which could be used to walk.

Just past the steepest part of the hill, fork off **to the L** by the golf club, and **keep L** at the next fork to arrive at a T-junction with the main road through Flackwell Heath. **Turn L** and then **first R** onto Chapman Lane. This turns into a narrow single track road, just after

passing Green Dragon Lane, and descends steeply into the Thames Valley at Well End. **Bear R** with the road at the minor junction at the bottom of the hill, and then follow the road through a 90-degree left bend to a T-junction with the A4155 Bourne End to Marlow road.

Turn R with care and follow this busy road for a short distance to a L-**hand turn** signed for Spade Oak. Take this for a recommended detour to the Spade Oak pub, and a delightful stretch of Thamesside meadow. Return then to the main road and **turn L** onto the shared-use cycle path on the left side of the road. On entering Little Marlow, **turn L** onto School Lane to a junction just past the cricket field on the right.

Straight on leads to Pound Lane and the delightfully sited Queen's Head, but the route **turns R** and passes the King's Head to return to the main road and cycleway. **Turn L** and then cross to the shared-use path on the opposite side via the central island and continue to Winchbottom Lane. **Turn R** here and after 1½ miles at a junction follow the road **to the L** by a farm, signed Handy Cross, and then shortly **turn R** onto an unnamed minor lane, marked as a 'no through road' and signed as a footpath.

This leads to a dead end, shortly after passing a gated road to the left, and a flight of steep steps up to Heath End road. Continuing on the path avoids the steep climb up the steps, but is often overgrown. **Turn L** at the road, cross the M40 bridge, then **turn R** onto the road into Daws Hill air base. **Take care**, as this road can be busy. Do not follow the road into the air base, but **turn immediately R** on a narrow track between fences, which is an old county

Cycleway along the Rye at High Wycombe

road. This track then bends left to pass between fences separating the air base from its accommodation. As the air base is left behind, the track steepens and descends as a bridleway, quite steep in places, through woodland to reach a road and the junction where the route left the cycle path behind the Rye earlier in the day.

The path through the Rye is then followed back to High Wycombe, reversing the outward journey.

PANN MILL

Pann Mill seen near the beginning of this route has recently restarted grinding corn, having been lovingly restored by the High Wycombe Society. Most of Pann Mill had been demolished in 1972 in order to facilitate road widening.

HIGH WYCOMBE

High Wycombe is probably best known for its furniture trade, examples of which can be seen in the Wycombe Local History and Chair Museum on Priory Avenue (open Mondays to Saturdays except Bank Holidays). The town grew up on this business which relied heavily on the skills of bodgers who lived in the woods a long way from the nearest villages. Here they felled trees, sawed the trunks and made chair legs, seats, arms and backs to sell on to the chair makers of Wycombe.

The Rye is a popular recreational area for local people to play football, walk, cycle, and even swim in the outdoor pool, built on the site of an old Roman villa in 1957. It also provides the venue for large community events that are now commonplace in this multicultural town, such as Wycombe Annual Show, the Caribbean Carnival and the Asian Mela.

From the middle ages until the early 18th century the Chiltern Hills provided a refuge for cut-throats and highwaymen who preyed on travellers of the great road between London and Oxford, passing through High Wycombe. A Steward of the Chiltern Hundreds was appointed to catch and hang as many of these rogues as possible. Bizarrely this position still exists today and is filled by MPs wishing to resign from their parliamentary duties prior to standing down in the next election!

16

Burnham Beeches and Beyond

13½ miles

A ride on quiet lanes and tracks that begins at one of the beauty spots of the Chilterns. Burnham Beeches is a picturesque remnant of the woods which once clothed this area, its glades and ancient pollarded beeches now protected for our enjoyment. Beautiful at any time of the year but spectacular in autumn. The route then passes a Farm Park and skirts the impressive Cliveden estate, returning through the village of Burnham. Burnham Beeches is owned by the Corporation of London, and is a very popular day out for locals and visitors alike. It is also frequently used as a film and TV set location and crews with their entourage of vehicles are often seen.

Map: OS Landranger 175 Reading and Windsor or OS Explorer 172 (GR 956850).

Starting point: There is good parking in the Beeches alongside the open space to the east on Beeches Way, most easily accessed from the A355 Beaconsfield to Slough road in Farnham Common.

By train: The nearest railway station is Burnham, on the London Paddington to Reading line.

Refreshments: Close to the parking near Victory Cross there is a very good refreshment hut, The Glade, serving drinks and snacks, and which is open all year. The Dell, another refreshment hut, is by the entrance via Lord Mayor's Drive, toilets are also located nearby. Several pubs are passed en route once outside the Beeches, the Three Feathers, by Cliveden, being of particular note. On arriving back at the Beeches, the closest pub is the Stag, which is approximately ¼ mile past the entrance at Lord Mayor's Drive. The route also passes through Burnham which has many shops and all facilities.

The route: Only the tarmac roads are currently open to cyclists in the Beeches, and this route explores those before venturing out onto the surrounding lanes. Off-road cycling in the Beeches is a sensitive issue, it was once allowed but thoughtless mountain bikers riding without care and consideration for others and the environment meant the 'no cycling' signs went up. One day more access may be allowed, but in the meantime stick to the tarmac unless there is a clear indication that things have changed and a particular route is now open to cycles.

From the parking **turn R** and follow Beeches Way back to the edge of the Beeches. **Turn L** onto Stewart Drive, and follow this lane for ½ mile. Then

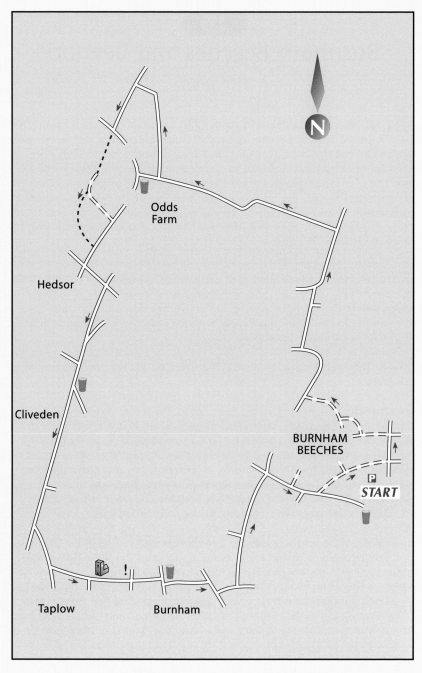

Odds
Farm

Hedsor

Cliveden

BURNHAM
BEECHES

START

Taplow

Burnham

turn L at a small crossroads, with The Avenue to the right, to re-enter the Beeches by Dukes Drive. The drive descends into a small valley, and on climbing out the other side where the road levels off, take the **first R** onto McAuliffe Drive. After bending to the left this road leads to a junction, where **turn R** by Hartley Court Moat onto Morton Drive to shortly arrive at the edge of the woods and Park Lane.

Turn R and follow Park Lane for just over ½ mile, where, shortly after a sharp left bend, **turn R** onto Abbey Park Lane signed to Beaconsfield. At a 'Give Way', just after passing Harehatch Lane to the right, **turn R** to continue in the same general direction. At the bottom of a steep hill, and hidden by the edge of the woods on the left, **turn L** onto Green Common Lane, opposite a public footpath sign. This junction is very easy to miss.

After just over 1 mile arrive at a minor junction with Odds Farm on the left and other farm buildings to the right by a small pond. **Turn R** here, or to visit the farm or the Royal Standard public house (with food and garden), continue to the end of the lane and **turn L**, before returning to continue the route.

Continue now on this lane, through a 90 degree left bend to a more major road where **turn L** heading back towards Odds Farm. At the next junction, leave the road to continue straight ahead on a bridleway that runs alongside the lane leading to The Chase. This can be a little muddy, but not normally anything to worry about. Emerge on the private road of Bergers Hill.

Where the private road bends to the left, the bridleway continues along a narrow path under the overhanging gable of a house to the right. This bridleway again can be muddy, more so than the previous section. If required **turn L** and follow the private road to the main road and **turn R**, otherwise follow the bridleway and where it arrives back at the road, **turn R**. Either way, shortly arrive at a crossroads in Hedsor. **Turn L** onto Hedsor Lane, follow this to the next road junction, where **turn R** onto Sheepcote Lane.

Keep R at the next junction, pass Bourne End Road on the right, and in ¾ mile pass the main entrance to Cliveden on the right, opposite the Three Feathers pub. **Keep R** here, pass Huntswood Lane on the left, and then **turn L** onto Hill Farm Road just past the white gatehouse at the end of Cliveden's Green Drive, and just before the woodland car park. There is limited cycle parking here and access to Cliveden.

The route shortly arrives in Taplow, where **turn L** onto Hitcham Lane on entering the village. Follow the lane for approximately 1 mile, ignoring a right-hand turn just before the church. This leads to a crossroads with double mini-roundabouts. Continue straight ahead **with care** into Burnham. After ½ mile go straight on at a slightly staggered junction at the top of the High Street. A little further on **turn L** onto Brickwell Road towards Farnham Royal, and then **first L** onto Green Lane.

This lane is now followed for approximately 1½ miles to a 'Give Way' at the edge of the Beeches. **Turn R** here and descend Pumpkin Hill, passing Victoria Drive on the left. A

Cycling along a carpet of beech leaves in winter sunshine

short climb then leads past Grove Lane to the right, to the Lord Mayor's Drive **on the** L leading into the Beeches. Follow this for ½ mile through the woods to arrive back at the starting point.

• •

BURNHAM BEECHES

Burnham Beeches is a large area of woodland which was purchased for use by the public 'forever' by the Corporation of London in 1880. The wonderful gnarled appearance of the trees is a result of years of pollarding, which was in operation up until coal replaced wood as the main fuel source in the early 1800s. The wood was turned into charcoal and used to fuel the fires and fogs of London. (See Route 7 for more on beech woods.)

CLIVEDEN

The spectacular estate of Cliveden overlooks the River Thames and was once the home of Nancy, Lady Astor. The estate, garden and three rooms of the house are open to the public during the summer months. However, the main portion of the house is now a hotel, and concerts and open air theatre take place in the spectacular grounds.

ODDS FARM PARK

Odds Farm Park is one of 20 approved rare breeds' centres in the country. It is

Bridleway, Bergers Hill

open most of the year and is designed with children in mind, offering tractor rides around the farm and theme days eg sheepdog days, and pumpkin lantern making. Other attractions include a tea room, gift shop, fitness trail and picnic area.

Cowleaze Wood and Christmas Common

13 miles

A short, relatively easy circuit in the heart of red kite country, with only one major climb to contend with but some spectacular views. Starting from the Forestry Commission's Cowleaze Wood, with its Sculpture Trail and woodland walks, and visiting Aston Rowant Nature Reserve, a restored windmill, and the village which was the setting for *The Vicar of Dibley*, interest is maintained throughout.

Maps: OS Landranger 165 Aylesbury and Leighton Buzzard and 175 Reading and Windsor or OS Explorer 171 (GR 727957).

Starting point: The route starts from Cowleaze Wood where there is ample parking. This is most easily reached from the A40 near Stokenchurch, taking the minor road heading for Christmas Common.

By train: There is no railway station nearby.

Refreshments: There are no facilities on the outward route, but a trio of excellent pubs in Turville, Northend and Christmas Common offer plenty of opportunity for refreshment on the homeward leg.

The route: For the more ambitious, this route links with Route 18 as a figure of eight to give a long ride.

From the car park **turn R** and follow the road to cross over the M40. Shortly after this, and at the edge of woodland, take a **L-hand turn** to visit the Aston Rowant Nature Reserve. Return then to the road and **turn L** to a 'Give Way' at a junction with the A40 where **turn R**.

At the next 'Give Way' **turn R**, signed for Ibstone and the motorway, to re-cross the M40; **take care** as this is an exit and entry junction for the M40 and so quite busy. Once past the M40 the road narrows and becomes much quieter.

Continue through woodland to Ibstone, passing the Fox restaurant and hotel on the left, and the common on the right. Ignore minor right turns, and continue with unfolding views to a steep descent to a junction.

Turn R, heading for Turville, ignore the left turn for Turville Heath and continue into Turville village, passing the Bull and Butcher pub. Pass a right turn, and continue signed for Northend, up the wooded valley bottom. The gradient eventually

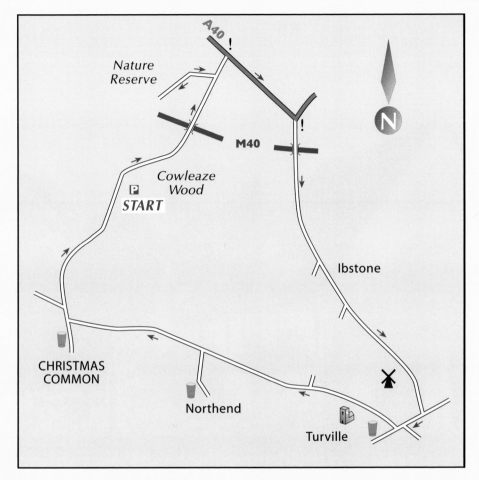

steepens for a long climb up a typical sunken Chiltern lane leading to a 'Give Way' in Northend. **Turn L** here for a visit to the White Hart, otherwise **turn R** heading for Christmas Common.

At the junction in Christmas Common, **turn L** to visit the Fox and Hounds, or **R** to continue the route proper. Ignore the left turn to Watlington and follow the road, with occasional glimpsed views away to the left, back to the car park.

COWLEAZE WOOD
Cowleaze Wood Sculpture Trail, the result of a collaboration between The Forestry Commission and the Chiltern Sculpture Trust, features two well laid out walking routes with a number of unusual sculptures positioned within easy reach of the paths.

ASTON ROWANT NATURE RESERVE
Natural England's Aston Rowant Nature Reserve is adjacent to the M40 motorway's famous cutting in the chalk. The fact that the motorway would cut through this prime chalk downland site

The Bull and Butcher pub, Turville

was a key issue in the unsuccessful campaign to stop or re-route the motorway.

COBSTONE WINDMILL
High above Turville stands Cobstone Windmill, a fine example of a smock mill, that is a tower mill with twelve tapering timber sides. It was restored in the 1980s and is now privately owned and so not open to the public.

RED KITES
By the middle of the 19th century red kites had become very rare in Buckinghamshire, but the 1980s saw a

Turville – 'Vicar of Dibley' country

slight natural increase, with six birds sighted over the Chiltern Escarpment. An organised release scheme in 1989 by the RSPB and English Nature (now known as Natural England) means that it is now unusual not to see a red kite in much of this area, but it is always a thrilling sight.

Henley and Skirmett

18½ miles

Breweries, vineyards and a punning pub are some of the features of this tough circuit from the Regatta town. There are many attractions in Henley, and it is well worth taking some time after the ride to explore and wander along the riverside. Other sights to look out for on the way are Turville windmill, away on the skyline, and the impressive mausoleums in Fawley churchyard.

Map: OS Landranger 175 Reading and Windsor or OS Explorer 171 (GR 767821).

Starting point: There is plenty of parking in Henley, and the route is described from the riverside car park by the River and Rowing Museum, and adjacent to the railway station. There is a café and toilets by the car park as well as access to the riverside and museum. The car park is very popular and, especially on Sundays, arrive early if you want to get a space.

By train: Henley on Thames station is on the Reading to Henley line.

Refreshments: Henley is a busy town with many bars, restaurants and shops. Several pubs are passed on the route, but the Frog at Skirmett and the Walnut Tree at Fawley are recommended, both have good beer, excellent food, a garden and a very pleasant location.

The route: A route of steep climbs and descents but rewarded by excellent views and delightful, quiet, hilltop and valley bottom lanes – a world away from the hustle and bustle of Thamesside Henley where the route starts.

Go to the far end of the car park, past the River and Rowing Museum, to where it meets the river, and **turn L** onto the riverside path. This is often very busy with pedestrians, and it may be best to dismount and walk. At the road **turn L**, pass Meadow Road (leading back to the car park), and then the railway station and at the mini-roundabout **turn R** heading into the Town Centre.

Go straight on at two sets of traffic lights to arrive on Bell Street. At the mini-roundabouts, **bear L** on the 'A' road heading for Wallingford. **Cross the road with care** near the Old White Horse, to join the shared-use cycle path on the right. Where the cycle path ends at a junction, **turn R** into Lower Assendon, and very shortly **L** onto a minor lane signed as 'unsuitable for HGVs'. A long gradual climb leads into Bix, where **turn R** at the junction by the church.

Follow the road through a sharp right bend where Bix Common, 'no through

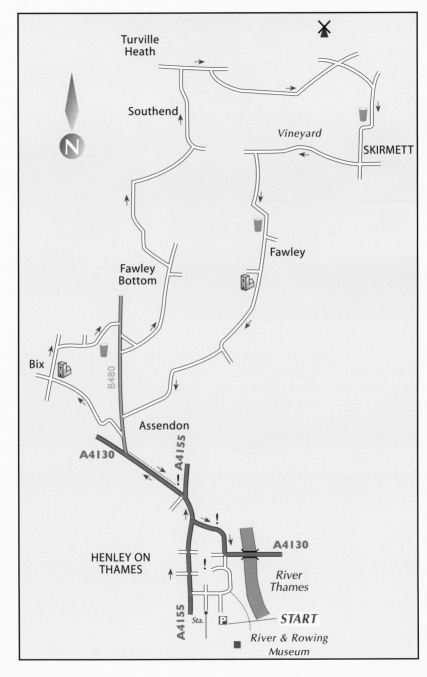

Turville Heath

Southend

Vineyard

SKIRMETT

Fawley Bottom

Fawley

Bix

B480

Assendon

A4130

A4155

HENLEY ON THAMES

A4130

River Thames

A4155

Sta.

START

River & Rowing Museum

N

Boats and bikes on the Thames at Henley

road', goes straight ahead. Ignore the left turn onto Rectory Lane and follow White Lane and descend steeply after a sharp left-hand bend. **Turn R** at the 'Give Way' and shortly **L** and then **L again** by the Rainbow Inn, heading for Fawley. Keep with the lane as it climbs and dips up Fawley Bottom. Ignore a right turn for Fawley and then **keep L** by the Old Bakehouse where a 'no through road' goes straight on to Bosmore Farm and Jackson's Farmhouse. A long climb now follows, steep in parts, to emerge on the hilltop with good views to the right and behind.

At a junction **turn L** for Southend, and after passing through this small hamlet, **turn R** at a junction on the edge of Turville Heath. Descend now, ignoring a 'no through road' to the left, initially steeply but then more

gently between open fields with views across to Turville windmill on the left. After a sharp left bend, arrive at a 'Give Way' and **turn R**, and almost immediately **R again** onto the traffic prohibited Watery Lane.

Turn R at the end of this lane, to pass the Frog in Skirmett and follow the road as it bends right and then left leaving the village. At a crossroads **turn R**, signed for the Chiltern Valley Winery and Brewery, climb steeply and then more gently through woodland. Pass vineyards on the right near the top of the hill, and then the car park and buildings of the winery and brewery. At a junction **turn L**, heading for Fawley and Henley.

Descend and then climb briefly through sharp bends to pass the Walnut Tree pub and restaurant in

Fawley. Ignore a left turn to Marlow, and after passing the village hall **bear L** at a fork by the church. In ½ mile at a sharp left bend, signed Henley to the left, **turn R** on a narrow lane – easy to miss.

After a sharp left bend, the lane starts a long and steep descent, **take care** – there is often loose gravel on the road, and bends that can hide approaching cars. At the 'Give Way' **turn L**, and at the next junction join the shared-use cycle path followed on the outward journey.

Rejoin the road where the cycleway finishes, just before the mini-roundabouts. Go across the roundabouts, signed for Reading and heading into Henley, and **turn L** with the road to pass the Brakspear Brewery on the right and to arrive at the riverside. Keep in the right-hand lane now, heading for Reading. Go straight on at the traffic lights, and **keep L** where a road joins from the right.

Where the road bends away from the river either return along the riverside path, or take the **first L** back into the car park, or if travelling by train, the second left to the rail station.

HENLEY

Henley is probably best known for its Regatta, which is held in the first week of July and attracts crews and visitors from all over the world. Not so well known is that the first ever Oxford and Cambridge boat race took place at Henley in 1829 (Cambridge lost!). The Regatta was also first held in 1829 and earned its 'Royal' title in 1851, courtesy of Prince Albert. The River and Rowing Museum found at the beginning of our route, is the only museum of its kind in the world dedicated to rowing and the 'quest for speed'. It is open every day except Christmas and New Year and has a shop, café and free visitor car park.

OLD LUXTERS VINEYARD, BREWERY AND GALLERY

Well worth a visit, the site is open almost every day and you can sample the locally grown and produced Chiltern Valley wines and beer. With its stone courtyard, and traditional barn this makes a popular venue for functions and themed musical dinners. There are also a local jeweller, art gallery and cellar shop on site.

FAWLEY CHURCHYARD

The churchyard at Fawley houses two impressive family mausoleums, one dating back to 1750 for the Freemans, and one erected in 1862 for the Mackenzies. The church itself was restored in 1883 for John Freeman of Fawley Court.

19

Stoke Row and Checkendon

12½ miles

A route on little used lanes to visit a Maharajah's gift to the southern Chilterns at Stoke Row, and a small zoo in a surprising location.

Map: OS Landranger 175 Reading and Windsor or OS Explorer 171 (GR 704813).

Starting point: A small crossroads near the shop in Peppard (the old post office) by the bus stop and just off Gallowstree Road. Best approached from the B481, where it is a left turn in Peppard on the Stoke Row road, if coming from Reading.

By train: The nearest railway station at Henley on Thames is approximately 5 miles to the east.

Refreshments: There are several pubs near the start in the Rotherfield Peppard area and also in Stoke Row. Near the end and just off route, the Four Horseshoes in Checkendon is very pleasant with good food.

The route: A relatively easy ride in the wooded heart of the Oxfordshire Chilterns with very little traffic to contend with, an ideal family trip.

From the crossroads, go over onto Gallowstree Road and then **turn R** onto the rough track of Chiltern Road. **Turn R** at the end of this track and at the junction go straight across and **turn L** in front of the Unicorn onto Colmore Lane. The road turns to track by Burnt Platt Wood, where continue straight ahead.

Where the track emerges back at a road, **turn L**. **Keep L** at a sharp bend and climb through woodland into Stoke Row. Pass the common and Cherry Tree pub, and note opposite the village hall the Maharajah's Well on the right.

Pass the Checkendon turn, and

National Cycle Network Route 5 turn for Wallingford, and take the **next L** signed for Ipsden and Wellplace Zoo. Go straight across the crossroads, gently descending, before a steeper section leads to a junction with a 'no through road' to the right by the entrance to Wellplace Zoo, **turn L** here.

Arrive in Ipsden and at a crossroads **turn L**, signed for Ipsden and Woodcote. Go straight on at a right turn for Ipsden, now following the National Cycle Network Route 5. Go straight across at the next crossroads heading for Braziers Park, pass minor turns and then the entrance to Braziers College, and at the next junction **turn L** opposite a bridleway.

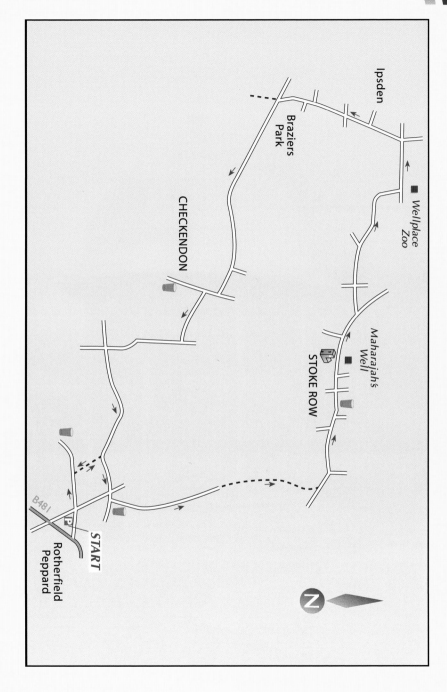

The Maharajah's Well is testament to a special friendship

Wind gently up the valley, and then more steeply following a sharp right bend by houses. At the 'Give Way' **turn R** heading for Checkendon, and at the next 'Give Way', **turn R** and then **L** onto Whitehall Lane. Pass a junction with a bridleway and descend through woodland.

At the 'Give Way' **turn R**, then in approximately 1 mile, at a crossroads **turn L**. Pass Wyfold Farm and just before the end of Wyfold Lane, and by the 30 mph speed limit sign, **turn R** onto the rough track of Chiltern Road that was followed on the outward journey. **Turn L** at the end to return to the starting point.

MAHARAJAH'S WELL

The ornate Maharajah's Well found in Stoke Row is appropriately named. In the 1850s, Edward Reade was governor of the North West provinces of India and struck up a friendship with the Maharajah of Benares. Edward told the Maharajah of the problems that this Chiltern village endured in obtaining water during the summer, being forced to collect it from ponds and ditches, and how children were beaten for stealing a drink! The Maharajah was so touched by this story that he immediately donated sufficient funds to dig the well, and so it remains as a testament to this special friendship.

WELLPLACE ZOO

The Zoo is open every day in the summer and weekends only in winter. It provides a pleasant diversion for the children and also has a sheltered picnic area and small café.

NATIONAL CYCLE NETWORK

The Sustrans National Cycle Network Route 5 links Oxford to Reading, where it joins Route 4, in combination with which it forms the 'Thames Valley Cycle Route' – a 97 mile route from London to Oxford.

Goring and the Thames Path

18 miles

Hilltop woodland and riverside settlements where the Thames separates the Chilterns from the Berkshire Downs are explored on this ride. The route starts out along the River Thames to Mapledurham, with its grand house, watermill and country park, before climbing to the hilltop village of Woodcote and then descending to finish on more Thamesside bridleway. An excellent 'all round' cycle ride.

Map: OS Landranger 175 Reading and Windsor or OS Explorer 171 (GR 602806).

Starting point: From Goring railway station where there is good parking (fee payable), not restricted to rail users.

By train: Goring and Streatley station is on the London Paddington to Reading line.

Refreshments: Goring itself is a popular tourist spot, with plenty of pubs, restaurants and shops. Recommended pubs along the route are the King Charles at Goring Heath, the Red Lion at Woodcote (by the common) and the Perch and Pike in South Stoke. There is also a small supermarket in Woodcote.

The route: This is a long and relatively strenuous ride with plenty of good off-road sections.

Turn R out of the station car park and in ½ mile **turn R** again signed for Gatehampton Nurseries and Gatehampton Manor. By the nursery **bear L** signed 'No Entry, Access Only' onto the bridleway heading for Whitchurch. Follow the blue signs of the Thames Path bridleway, climbing gradually above the Thames until a final steep climb leaves the woods and arrives at a flight of steps into and out of a small valley. **Take care here.**

Continue straight ahead on the farm road to join the B471 near Whitchurch on Thames. **Turn R** onto this road and

very shortly **L** onto Hardwick Road. Pass Bozedown Vineyard and Farm, and shortly at a left-hand bend leave the road through iron gates to continue straight on, signed as a bridle road for Caversham, and marked as a private road. Follow this road past Hardwick Stud and House, until at the end of the road **keep L** to stay with the bridle track and maintain the same general direction, ignoring the private drive directly ahead. At another set of metal gates go straight on, onto a rougher bridleway leading to the road in Mapledurham. **Turn R** to visit Mapledurham House.

The old mill, Mapledurham

An enchanting glimpse of the river from the Thames Path

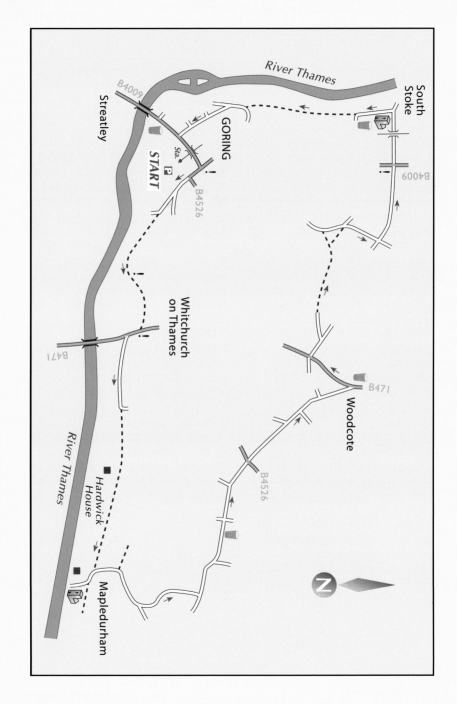

Return from Mapledurham passing the bridle road and **keep R** past the track to Bottom Farm. Then start to climb from the Thames, **keeping L** at a junction, and **turning L** at a more major road.

Pass the King Charles and go straight on at the crossroads, and at a four-way junction, straight on to Long Toll as the main road bends to the left. This climbs up to Woodcote and is followed all the way to a junction with Goring Road on the edge of the common. If a visit to the Red Lion pub is desired **turn R** here, otherwise **turn L**.

At a staggered junction **turn R** onto Beech Lane and then shortly **L** to stay on Beech Lane, signed 'no through road'. This turns into a rough track, which can be muddy in places but mainly rideable. Continue straight ahead until after approximately 1½ miles, meet a road and **turn R**. Ignore a minor left, and in just over ½ mile reach a four-way junction, where **turn L** onto Woodcote Road, signed for South Stoke.

At the B4009 go straight across, under the railway and **turn first L**. Where the road bends left go straight ahead onto the Ridgeway bridleway.

The bridleway becomes gravel track and then tarmac, passing through houses before again turning to bridleway where the road goes down to the Leatherne Bottle. The bridleway

then leads to another gravel track by houses before coming to a road on a sharp bend, where go straight ahead on Cleeve Road. Ignore right-hand Glebe Ride to stay on Cleeve Road and at the junction with the main road in Goring, **turn R** to visit the village, or **L** over the railway bridge and then **R** to return to the station car park.

● ●

BOZE DOWN VINEYARD
This vineyard at Whitchurch on Thames was first planted in 1985. Six varieties of white grape and four red are grown here. It used to make and sell its own wine but now concentrates on supplying its grapes to other English vineyards. The grass verges found around the vineyard are home to a colourful variety of wild flowers.

MAPLEDURHAM
The House, Watermill and Country Park are open to the public on most weekends and Bank Holidays in the summer. Sir Richard Blount built the house as a family home in 1585, its imposing wrought iron gateway leading to the 14th century churchyard that provides the final resting place for members of the family. The 15th century mill is one of the last on the banks of the River Thames to produce flour, and is still kept in working order.

FURTHER INFORMATION

As you get more involved, you will probably want to keep up to date with what is happening locally and nationally on the cycling scene. The popular press is dominated by mountain bike magazines, but more all round titles, notably *Cycling Plus*, do exist and are a good starting point for national information. Most good newsagents will stock a suitable title.

The National Cycling Network has been big news in recent years, and Sustrans – the sustainable transport charity driving this – are active locally as well as nationally. Their web site and newsletters provide an overview and updates on the network, and maps and books cover the detail. The major route passing through the Chilterns is Route 5, the Thames Valley route from Reading to Oxford.

There are many other cycle routes within or close to the Chilterns, check out local tourist information shops for details, maps and guides.

The Chiltern Society, an environmental charity, is involved in local planning and rights of way issues, and also has a cycling group whose activities include organised rides.

Nationally, the Cycle Touring Club (CTC) is the largest cycling organisation and local groups in the Chilterns organise rides and social events.

Contact Details:

Sustrans: 2 Cathedral Square, College Green, Bristol, BS1 5DD
www.sustrans.org.uk

Chiltern Society: White Hill Centre, White Hill, Chesham, HP5 1AG
www.chilternsociety.org.uk

CTC: Cotterell House, Parklands, Railton Road, Guildford,
Surrey, GU2 9JX
www.ctc.org.uk